KANNIBALS, KILLERS, KULTS AND KINKERY

THE BRAVINSKI FAMILY

MILTON & HUGO L.L.C.
4407 Park Ave., Suite 5
Union City, NJ 07087, USA

Website: www. miltonandhugo.com
Hotline: 1- 888-778-0033
Email: info@miltonandhugo.com

Ordering Information:
Quantity sales. Special discounts are available on quantity purchases by corporations, associations, and others. For details, contact the publisher at the address above.

Library of Congress Control Number: 2024920736
ISBN-13:   979-8-89285-284-5   [Hardback Edition]
                  979-8-89285-285-2   [Digital Edition]

Rev. date: 09/30/2024

KANNIBALS, KILLERS, KULTS AND KINKERY

THE BRAVINSKI FAMILY

FOREWORD

Throughout human history there have been two constant forces that, until now, have been kept apart as a matter of appropriateness. One is the creativity of new recipes and experimenting with new combinations of ingredients. The other is the destruction of serial killers, mass murderers, and the criminally insane. The recipes found in this book are a play on classic recipes with directions, ingredients, and names of dishes based on killers, madmen, charismatic sociopaths, sexual deviants, and cults of personality, both real and fictional throughout the history of mankind.

The idea for this cookbook came to us as we were having two divergent conversations as a family. We were watching true crime documentaries while cooking and the idea was sparked. Over time we developed new ideas and new names for classic dishes. This book started as a thought provoking idea of how kannibals know how to eat human flesh and became the wonder that it is now. Please enjoy the information in this book and the food that the recipes will help you produce.

The Bravinski Family

TABLE OF CONTENTS

Recipe	Chapter	Inspiration	Ode name
Pork Belly	Kannibals	Sawney Bean	Top to Bottom Pork Belly
Chicken al la King	Kannibals	Jeffrey Dahmer	Cream of Sum Yung Guey
Salisbury Steak	Kannibals	Peruvian Soccer Team	Stewardess Thigh Steak w/ Mint Garnish
Bourbon Chicken	Kannibals	Levi Boone Helm	Helm's Bourbon Chicken Legs
Braised Ribs	Kannibals	Alfred Packer	Packer's Golden Ribs
Shrimp Scampi	Kannibals	SS Dumaru	Dumaru Scampi
Open faced Chili Size	Kannibals	Rudy Eugene	Rudy's Open Face Chili Burger
Garden Stew	Kannibals	Elizabeth Wright	John Stew with Garden Veggies
Eggs Benedict	Kannibals	Donner Party	Poached Ovaries with Toddler Sauce
Liver and Onions	Kannibals	Hannibal Lechter	Lechter's Liver and Onions w/Chiante
Manicotti	Killers	The Menendez Brothers	Double Barrel Manicoti
Orange Citrus Bundt Cake	Killers	Ted Bundy	Bundy Bundt Cake
Stuffed and Tied Pork Loin	Killers	BTK	Bound and Stuffed Loin
Cotton Candy Cake Pops	Killers	John Wayne Gacy	Play with the Sweet Clown
Zen Kus Kus Salad	Killers	Zodiac	Can You Solve It?
Beef Enchiladas	Killers	Night Stalker	Satan's Enchilada
Chicken and Noodles	Killers	Son of Sam	Son of Sam Chicken and Noodle Yada Yada
Herb Crusted Pork Loin	Killers	Manson Family	Mansons Favorite Loin
Canolli	Killers	Peter Clemenza	Leave the gun. Take the canolli.

Pulled BBQ Pork	Killers	Jack the Ripper	Ripped Off the Bone Butt
Little Weenies and Meatballs	Kinkery	Elmer McGurdy	McGurdy's Encased Meats
Twice Baked Potato	Kinkery	Mae West	Don't Bake it Once, Bake it Twice
Whipped Pineapple Cream	Kinkery	Christian Gray	WHIPPED Pineapple Cream
Beef Tips and Noodles	Kinkery	Betty Paige	Tastiest Leather and Lace
Mini Devils Food Cakes	Kinkery	Jessica Rabbit	Patty Cake Patty Cake
Lemon Chifon Cake	Kinkery	Marilyn Monroe	Marilyn's Lemon Lingerie Cake
Cream Puff	Kinkery	Madame Du Berry	King's Cortisan Puff
Pink Champagne Cake	Kinkery	Moulan Rouge	Pink Rouge
Chocolate Raspberry Brownies	Kinkery	Lady Chatterly	Lady Chatterly's Dark Secret
Indian Delights	Kinkery	Madahari	Madahari's Sinful Sensation
Cherry Pie	Kinkery	Hester Prynn	Puritan Cherry Pie
Kool-Aid Cookies	Kults	People's Temple	Jim's Kool-Aid Treat
Chicken Wings	Kults	Heavens Gate	Heavens Hellishly Hot Wings
Burnt Ends	Kults	Branch Davidians	Davidians Burnt End
Multi-Layered Cake	Kults	Nxivm	Ranier's Racketeering Cake
Angels Food Cake	Kults	Angels Landing	Fallen Angel Food Cake
Corn Bread	Kults	Children of God	Children of the Cornbread
Spaghetti and Meatsauce	Kults	Matamoros	Ritual Sacrifice with Spaghetti
Monte Cristo	Kults	Order of the Solar Temple	Knights Templar's Maybe Monte Cristo
Beef and Cheese Enchiladas	Kults	Movement for the Restoration of the Ten Commandments of God	Fire and Brimstone Chili and Cornbread
Terriyaki Chicken w/ Steamed Rice	Kults	Aum Shinrikyo	Sarin Chicken w/ White Rice

I.
KANNIBALS

Sawney Bean

Sawney Bean, believed to be born in the late 15th century, was a tanner from East Lothian who settled in Ayrshire with his wife in Bennane Cave. Utilizing robbery as a means of income, he progressed to murdering travelers to prevent identification, then butchering their bodies for food. This gruesome practice led to the birth of 14 children, each raised on a diet of human flesh. Through generations, the family perfected their cannibalistic practices within the cave, evading suspicion and producing a long list of missing persons in the area.

As the family grew, so did their appetite, resulting in organized attacks on victims to meet their dietary needs. However, their downfall came when a group of witnesses stumbled upon an attack, prompting a manhunt led by King James I with a small army. Eventually, the family was discovered in Bennane Cave, where the troops found a horrifying scene of human body parts and belongings strewn about.

TOP TO BOTTOM PORK BELLY PORK BELLY BURNT ENDS

ODE TO SAWNEY BEAN

3 lbs of pork belly cubed into 1" pieces
2 Tablespoons of Smoked Paprkika
2 Tablespoons of Garlic Powder
1 Teaspoon of Crushed Red Pepper
½ Teaspoon of Seasoning Salt
¼ Teaspoon of Smoked Hickory Salt
¼ cup honey (optional)
½ cup of brown sugar (optional)
1/8 cup of bacon grease
Honey and brown sugar are for sweeter and for a caramelizing effect.

Combine all spices and toss the pork belly with the bacon grease. Place on smoker or grill with smoking packet for 3-4 hours. Check for doneness. 165 degrees. Remove and toss with choice of sauce, we use Sweet Baby Ray's. Wrap and return to heat for 1 hour. Remove and allow to rest for 30-45 minutes.

Jeffrey Dahmer

A sex offender, murdered 17 men and boys between 1978 and 1991. He was killed in prison in 1994. Dahmer's childhood was marked by trauma and withdrawal, leading to his fascination with animal bones. His crimes involved luring victims to his home, killing them, engaging in sexual acts with their corpses, and dismembering them. He stored body parts as souvenirs. Dahmer's first murder was in 1978, and he continued to kill until his arrest in 1991. He faced charges of sexual exploitation and second-degree sexual assault in 1989. Despite his crimes, Dahmer showed contrition during his trial in 1992. He was found guilty but sane and sentenced to multiple life terms in prison. Dahmer was killed in prison in 1994 by a fellow inmate.

Dahmer's crimes shocked the nation, and his arrest brought an end to his killing spree. The police discovered gruesome evidence in his apartment, including dismembered bodies and preserved body parts. Dahmer's infamy continued even after his death, with his childhood home being put on the market in 2012. His story has been depicted in various books, films, and documentaries, shedding light on the horrors of his actions.

CHICKEN ALA KING

C*M OF SUM YUNG GUYE

SAUCE

2 cups of shredded chicken (rotisserie makes it easy)
1 shredded carrot
1 celery stalk diced
1 potato peeled and diced
½ small onion diced
1 can cream of chicken
Salt and pepper to taste.

BISCUITS BAKE AT 400 DEGREES

2 cups of self-rising flour
1 cup of vegetable shortening
½ cup of buttermilk
Pinch of salt

Start with the biscuits. Place the flour and shortening in a bowl. Using your hands mix the shortening into the flour until it is completely incorporated and flour is grainy texture. Add salt and buttermilk. Continue to mix with hands. Mix until completely mixed together. DO NOT OVERMIX!. Place on a flour board. Pat down to ½"-3/4" thick. Use a 11/2" round cutter. Cut and place in a cast iron skillet or glass pan. Bake at 400 for approximately 10 minutes or until golden brown.

Sauce
Preheat skillet with butter until melted. Add vegetables and stir until almost tender. Add chicken and continue to stir. Add Salt and Pepper, then add cream of chicken soup and one can of water. Stir until all lumps are gone and mixture is bubbly. Split a biscuit and pour over the top.

Uruguay Rugby Team

On October 13, 1972, a chartered plane carrying an Uruguayan rugby team crashed in the Andes mountains. Only 16 out of the 45 passengers survived after enduring harsh conditions for two months. They resorted to cannibalism to survive.

Initially, the passengers remained calm as the plane experienced turbulence, but soon found themselves plummeting towards a mountain. After the crash, 29 survivors were left stranded, with no means of communication and dwindling food supplies. As days passed, they turned to consuming the flesh of their deceased companions to stay alive.

Eventually, a group of survivors decided to trek across the mountains in search of help. Despite their lack of mountaineering experience and proper equipment, they embarked on a perilous journey, facing extreme cold and altitude sickness. Their determination led them to encounter signs of civilization, and they finally attracted the attention of rescue teams by communicating through notes thrown across a river.

Rescuers arrived, initially skeptical of the survivors' incredible story, but eventually managed to locate and evacuate them. The survivors were brought to safety, where they received medical attention and nourishment after enduring unimaginable hardships.

The resilience and ingenuity displayed by the survivors in the face of adversity captured the world's attention, earning the event the title of the "Miracle of the Andes." The tale of their survival serves as a testament to the strength of the human spirit in the most dire circumstances.

STEWARDESS THIGH STEAK

SALISBURY STEAK

4-3-4 ounce slices of round steak
½ cup of flour
1 Egg
1 Tablespoon of Smoked Paprika
1 Tablespoon of Black Pepper
1 Teaspoon of Garlic Powder
16 ounce can of Stewed Tomatoes
1 Medium Onion
Vegetable Oil for browning

Using a meat mallet pound out round steak to ¼" thickness. Mix Flour, Paprika and Pepper together. Beat egg with ¼ cup of water. Dredge meat in flour, then egg and back in flour. Brown in vegetable oil and place in baking pan.

In the pan that meat was browned in add onions and garlic powder. Sautee until onions are tender and add Stewed tomatoes. Bring to a bubbling simmer. Pour over meat, lifting steaks to get in between. Cover and bake at 350 for 45 minutes. Let stand for 10 minutes, prior to serving.

Levi "Boone" Helm

"The Kentucky Cannibal" Levi Helm was known for robbery and murder prior to and during the American Civil War. On occasion he would also devour parts of his victims in order to hide the evidence of his crimes and for sustenance. Helm had a particular affinity for the thighs and calves of his victims. There are some who compare his killing and cannibalism to Jeffrey Dahmer, though there is no reliable evidence that Helm resorted to necrophilia in the way that Dahmer did.

Helm was captured, tried, convicted, and executed in Montana in 1864 after vigilante mob captured him and his gang in Montana. Helm tried to put some of the blame for his own crimes on other members of his gang, but it would not save his life. While on trial Helm sank any defense to his crimes when he stated "Many's the poor fool I've killed, at one time or another…and the time has been that I've been obliged to eat some of 'em".

While awaiting his turn to be hanged Helm reportedly remarked, as the man before him hanged, "Kick off old fellow. My turn next. I will be in Hell with you in a minute".

HELMS TASTY CHICKEN LEGS

BOURBON CHICKEN LEGS

One dozen chicken legs
2 Cups Bourbon
¼ cup honey
1 Teaspoon Garlic Powder
¼ cup lemon juice
Vegetable oil

Brown chicken legs in vegetable oil and place on a paper towel, drain off excess oil. In a saucepan, combine the bourbon, honey, garlic and lemon juice. Bring to a simmer and cook for 5 minutes. Pour mixture over chicken legs and turn the legs to coat on all sides. Cover with foil and bake at 350 degrees for 45 minutes. Uncover and bake for 15 minutes.

Alfred Packer

Alfred Packer enlisted twice in the Union Army during the American Civil War. He was honorably discharged both times with epilepsy. Packer went west to Colorado to prospect for gold and silver while working as a wilderness guide. On February 9, 1874 Packer left camp with five others to travel to Los Pinos Indian Agency. On April 16, 1874 Packer arrived alone at the agency looking surprisingly fit for someone that had completed a difficult trek through the Rocky Mountains in Eastern Colorado. When questioned about the missing men Packer stated that he had "got his feet wet and frozen", and the others had abandoned him.

Packer later confessed to having killed the other members of his party claiming self defense with each of the killings. The bodies of the other men were found to be at a single campsite after Packer consented to lead the investigators to the bodies, claimed to be lost, and rushed the constable with a knife. He broke out of jail and disappeared for nine years until March 11, 1883. Packer passed away at home April 23, 1907 of dementia at the age of 65. He was buried with full military honors in Littleton, CO.

PACKERS GOLDEN RIBS

ODE TO ALFRED PACKER

BRAISED SHORT RIBS

6-8 Short Ribs
1 Cup Worcestershire Sauce
1 Tablespoon Fresh Garlic
2 Tablespoons Heinz 57 Steak Sauce
1 Tablespoon Seasoning Salt
1 Tablespoon 1Black Pepper
Vegetable Oil

Season meat with dry ingredients. Brown the ribs in a skillet using the vegetable oil. Place the ribs in the baking dish. Mix the Worcestershire sauce and Heinz 57 sauce and pour over the ribs. Cover with foil and add 1 cup of water to the bottom of the pan and bake at 350 for 3 hours. Check for tenderness. Add an additional 30 minutes for increased tenderness. Uncover and bake an additional 30 minutes.

SS Dumaru

In September 1918, on its maiden voyage the 270 foot 1752-ton wooden SS Dumaru set sail from San Francisco on its way across the Pacific Ocean headed for Manila with stops in Hawaii and Guam. It was an ill-fated maiden voyage as the ship was not well-built and suffered from bad omens of seamen after colliding with several houseboats during its launch in Portland on April 17, 1918. The ship was carrying gasoline in its forward cargo hold and dynamite in the aft cargo hold. The Dumaru succeeded in making port in both Hawaii and Guam to deliver cargo.

On October 16 the Dumaru departed Apra Harbor in Guam for the final leg of its maiden voyage to Manila. About 20 miles out to sea from Guam the boat was struck by lightning setting off a chain reaction that would sink the ship, forcing all crew members to try for safety on one of two lifeboats or the small life raft. In the chaos and confusion of abandoning the ship the life vessels were not evenly distributed. One 20 man lifeboat carried only 9 while the other ended up with 32. After weeks afloat in the South Pacific the surviving 14 men made it ashore. The other 18 died of exposure and were cannibalized in order to keep the living men alive.

SHRIMP SCAMPI

SHRIMP SCAMPI

1 ½ lbs. of medium shrimp (peeled and veined)
- 2tablespoons butter
- 2tablespoons extra-virgin olive oil
- 1 tablespoon Old Bay Seasoning
- 4garlic cloves, minced
- ½cup dry white wine or broth
- ¾teaspoon kosher salt, or to taste
- ⅛teaspoon crushed red pepper flakes, or to taste
- Freshly ground black pepper
- ⅓ cup chopped parsley
- Freshly squeezed juice of one lemon
- Choice of pasta Linguine, angel hair or spaghetti are best

PREPARATION

Step 1
In a large skillet, melt butter with olive oil. Add garlic and sauté until fragrant, about 1 minute. Add wine or broth, salt, red pepper flakes and plenty of black pepper and bring to a simmer. Let wine reduce by half, about 2 minutes.

Step 2
Add shrimp and sauté until they just turn pink, 2 to 4 minutes depending upon their size. Stir in the parsley and lemon juice and serve over pasta or accompanied by crusty bread.

Rudy Eugene

On May 26, 2012, Rudy Eugene attacked and maimed Ronald Poppo, a homeless man, on the MacArthur Causeway in Miami, Florida. During the 18-minute filmed encounter, Eugene accused Poppo of stealing his Bible, beat him unconscious, removed his pants, and bit off most of Poppo's face above his beard (including his left eye), leaving him blind in both eyes. As a result of the incident's shocking nature and subsequent worldwide media coverage, Eugene came to be dubbed the "Miami Zombie" and the "Causeway Cannibal." The attack ended when Eugene was fatally shot by an officer of the Miami Police Department.

Although friends and family filled in details of Eugene's life, the reason for the attack remains unclear. Eugene, 31, employed at a car wash at the time, was divorced and had a series of petty criminal arrests from age 16, with the last in 2009. While police sources speculated that the use of a street drug like "bath salts" might have been a factor, experts expressed doubt, since toxicology reports were only able to identify small amounts of marijuana in Eugene's system, leaving the ultimate cause of his behavior unknown. Poppo, 65, a graduate of Manhattan's Stuyvesant High School, was homeless and had long been presumed dead by his estranged family.

OPEN FACED CHILI SIZE

OPEN FACED CHILI SIZE SANDWICH

4-1/3 lb. Hamburger Patties
Hamburger Buns
Grated Cheddar Cheese
Diced raw onion (to taste)

CHILI

1 lb. Ground Beef 80/20
½ lb. Ground pork or mild pork sausage
1 yellow onion diced small
1 small can tomato paste
1 12 ounce can tomato sauce, empty and fill with water
1 can Rotel tomatoes/green chilies
1 12 ounce can spicy V8 tomato juice
1 teaspoon garlic powder
2 Tablespoons chili powder
1 Tablespoon Smoked Paprika

Brown ground beef and pork and drain grease. Add all other ingredients and simmer for 1 hour. Add seasonings to taste.

Grill or Fry burgers while chili is cooking. Cook to 165 degrees. Toast hamburger buns and place open on a plate. Place the burger in the center of the buns. Ladle chili over the top, sprinkle cheese and onion over the top. Serve with fries, chips or other side.

Katherine Knight

On February 29, 2000, John Charles Thomas Price came home from work and followed his usual routine of checking in with the neighbors before going to bed at 11 p.m. Knight came home shortly after, made herself dinner, watched TV, showered, and then went upstairs. She woke Price, the two had sex, and he went back to bed.

Then, Katherine Knight took a butcher knife from next to her bed — where she had always kept them — and stabbed Price 37 times. According to evidence, he woke up during the attack but could not fight her off.

He succumbed to his wounds and Knight dragged his body downstairs, skinned him, and hung his body from a meat hook in the living room. Then, she decapitated him and cut up pieces of his body to cook in a dish with potato, pumpkin, beets, zucchini, cabbage, squash, and gravy. Knight also set bowls out for the children and set John's head to boil on the stove. She made a dish for herself, laid down to sleep under her husband's corpse. There she was found by police the next morning.

GARDEN STEW

ODE TOO KATHERINE KNIGHT

JOHN GARDEN VEGETABLE STEW

1 ½ lbs lean red meat (chuck roast or stew meat)
4-5 potatoes peeled and diced
1-2 carrots, peeled and diced
1-2 stalks of celery peeled and diced
1 small onion peeled and diced
2 small crowns of I
2 small crowns of cauliflower
1 cup of frozen or fresh peas
1 cup of frozen or fresh corn
1 large can of stewed tomatoes

Salt, pepper, garlic, flour, vegetable oil Onion soup mix, 2 cans of cream of mushroom soup.

Coat meat in flour and brown in vegetable oil. Add water and simmer for 11/2 to 2 hours on low or in a crock pot for 6 hours. Add vegetables and seasonings simmer until tender. Check carrots and broccoli. Check for taste and reseason if needed. Bring to a low boil and add cream of mushroom soup to thicken. Serve with birscuits or crusty bread.

The Donner Party

The Donner party left Springfield, Illinois, in April 1846. Led by two wealthy brothers, Jacob and George Donner, the emigrants initially followed the regular California Trail westward to Fort Bridger, Wyoming. From there, however, the emigrants decided to leave the established trail and take a new and supposedly shorter route to California laid out by an unscrupulous trail guide named Lansford Hastings. Hastings was not at Fort Bridger at the time—he was leading an earlier wagon train along his new route. He left word for the Donner party to follow, promising that he would mark the trail for them.

The Donner party finally made it through the Wasatch Mountains and arrived at the Great Salt Lake. Hastings' route had cost them 18 valuable days. Unfortunately, their difficulties were only beginning. The "shortcut" to California had cost them many wasted days, and the Donner party crossed the Sierra Nevada Mountains late in the season. On October 28, a heavy snowfall blocked the high mountain passes, trapping the emigrants in a frozen wilderness. Eventually reduced to cannibalism to survive—at least according to legend—only 45 of the original 89 emigrants reached California the following year.

EGGS BENEDICT

OVARIES WITH TODDLER SAUCE

INGREDIENTS FOR THE HOLLANDAISE SAUCE:

- 2 English muffins
- 4 large eggs
- 4 slices Canadian bacon
- Vinegar, just a splash

FOR THE HOLLANDAISE SAUCE:

- 4 Tablespoons butter
- 4 egg yolks
- 2 teaspoons lemon juice, or lime juice
- 1 Tablespoon heavy whipping cream
- salt and pepper (to taste)

For the Hollandaise sauce:

1. Melt the butter in a small saucepan. In a separate small bowl, beat the egg yolks. Mix in lemon juice, whipping cream, and salt and pepper.
2. Add a small spoonful of the hot melted butter to the egg mixture and stir well. Repeat this process adding a spoonful at a time of hot butter to the egg mixture. (Adding the butter slowly, a spoonful at a time, will temper the eggs and ensure they don't curdle).
3. Once the butter has been incorporated, pour the mixture back into the saucepan. Cook on low heat, stirring constantly, for just 20-30 seconds. Remove from heat and set aside. It will thicken as it cools. Stir well and add another splash of cream, if needed, to thin.

To poach the eggs:

1. Fill a medium size pot with about 3 inches of water. Bring the water to a boil and then reduce heat until it reaches a simmer. You should see small bubbles coming to the surface but not rolling.
2. Add a little splash of vinegar to the water (this is optional, but it helps the egg white to stay together once it is in the water).
3. Crack one egg into a small cup (I use a measuring cup). Lower the egg into the simmer water, gently easing it out of the cup.
4. Cook the egg in simmering water for 3-5 minutes, depending on how soft you want your egg yolk. Remove the poached egg with a slotted spoon.
5. **It is not abnormal for a white foam to form on top of the water when poaching an egg. You can simple skim the foam off of the water with a spoon.
6. While the egg is cooking, place the slices of Canadian bacon in a large pan and cook on medium-high heat for about 1 minute on each side.

To Assemble:

1. Toast the English muffin. Top each toasted side with a slice or two of Canadian bacon, and then a poached egg. Top with hollandaise sauce.

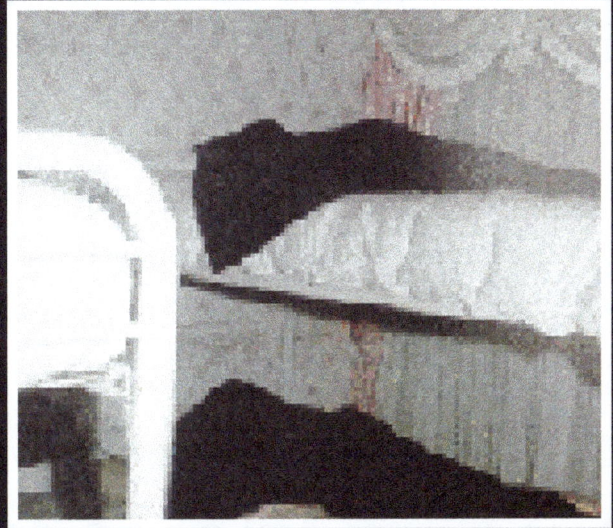

Hannibal Lecter

All media in which Lecter appears portray him as intellectually brilliant, cultured and sophisticated, with refined tastes in art, music and cuisine. He is frequently depicted preparing gourmet meals from his victims' flesh, the most famous example being his admission that he once ate a census taker's liver «with some fava beans and a nice Chianti" (a "big Amarone" in the novel). Prior to his capture and imprisonment, he was a member of Baltimore, Maryland's social elite, and a sitting member of the Baltimore Philharmonic Orchestra's Board of Directors.

In the novel *The Silence of the Lambs*, Lecter is described through Starling's eyes: "She could see that he was small, sleek; in his hands and arms she saw wiry strength like her own." The novel also reveals that Lecter's left hand has a rare condition called mid-ray duplication polydactyly, i.e. a duplicated middle finger. In *Hannibal*, he performs plastic surgery on his own face on several occasions, and removes his extra digit. Lecter's eyes are a shade of maroon, and reflect the light in "pinpoints of red". He has small white teeth and dark, slicked-back hair with a widow's peak. He has an eidetic memory with which he has constructed in his mind an elaborate «memory palace" to relive memories and sensations in rich detail.

LIVER AND ONIONS

LIVER AND ONIONS WITH CHIANTE

11/2 lbs. of fresh calf liver
8 strips of thick applewood bacon
1 medium onion
1 cup of flour
Salt and Pepper to taste in the flour
Chilled bottle of Chianti

Fry bacon to crisp and set aside. Calf liver should be sliced thin and flat. Dredge liver in flour and fry in bacon grease on one side until crispy and then flip to other side. Set on paper towel to drain. After cooking all the liver. Slice the onion Julienne strips and saute' in remaining grease. If needed, add additional butter and salt and pepper onions as they cook. Add the onions to the top of the liver and serve. Chianti should be served cold.

II.
KILLERS

The Menendez Brothers

On the evening of August 20, 1989, José and Kitty were standing in the den of their Beverly Hills mansion when Lyle and Erik entered the den, carrying shotguns. José was shot six times, including a fatal shot in the back of the head with a Mossberg 12-gauge shotgun. Kitty was shot ten times in total. Before the fatal shot to her cheek, she was on the ground, slowly crawling and crying. Lyle ran to his car to reload before firing the fatal shot to her face.

Immediately after the killings, both brothers remained in the house expecting the police to respond due to the noise of the gunshots. When the police arrived, the brothers told them that the killings had occurred while they were at a movie theater watching *Batman* and attending the «Taste of L.A.» festival at the Santa Monica Civic Auditorium.

In the months after the killings, the brothers began to spend extravagantly on luxury items, businesses, and travel. Lyle bought Chuck's Spring Street Cafe, a Buffalo wing restaurant in Princeton, New Jersey, as well as a Rolex watch and a Porsche Carrera. Erik hired a full-time tennis coach and competed in a series of tournaments in Israel. The brothers eventually left the Beverly Hills mansion unoccupied, choosing to live in adjoining condominiums in nearby Marina del Rey. They also dined expensively and took overseas trips to the Caribbean and London.

MANICOTTI

DOUBLE BARRELED MANICOTTI

10 manicotti
16 ounce ricotta cheese
3 cups mozzarella cheese divided
1/2 cup parmesan
1 cup spinach chopped into small pieces.
1 Tablespoon Italian seasoning
1 large egg

MARINARA SAUCE

2 Large cans of tomato sauce
1 Large can of Italian Stewed Tomatoes
2 Cans of Tomato Paste
2 Tablespoons of crushed garlic
4 Tablespoons Italian Seasoning

Place all ingredients in a crock pot along with a large

Can of water (from the tomato sauce) Cook on high for 3

Hours. Taste and season with salt and Italian Seasoning.

While sauce is cooking, boil manicotti noodles and set aside. Mix filling, and after noodles have cooled use a pastry bag with a cut end or Ziploc bag with cut corner to fill. Holding noodle pipe filling in just to full point and place in 9x13 pan. After sauce is done, pour over the top to cover, top with parmesan cheese, bake at 350 for 45 minutes.

Ted Bundy

Bundy confessed to murdering 30 women across several states in the 1970s, but experts believe that the final tally might be closer to 100 or more. After years of maintaining his innocence, Bundy's admission of guilt arrived just before his death. "It all felt like a ploy to extend his life," said former FBI agent Bill Hagmaier, who spent considerable time with the killer after he'd been caught.

There is some debate as to when Bundy started killing. Most sources say he began his murderous rampage around 1974. Around this time, many women in the Seattle area and in nearby Oregon went missing. Stories circulated about some of the victims last being seen in the company of a young, dark-haired man known as Ted.

His murders usually followed a gruesome pattern: He often raped his victims before beating them to death. Bundy often lured women into his car by pretending to be injured and asking for their help. Their kindness proved to be a fatal mistake.

ORANGE BUNDT CAKE

ODE TO TED BUNDY

BUNDY BUNDT CAKE

- 1 1/4 Cup Sugar
- 2 Tablespoons Orange Zest, about 2 oranges
- 1 Cup Fresh Orange Juice, 6-8 oranges juiced
- 3 Large Eggs
- 1 1/2 teaspoon Vanilla
- 1/4 teaspoon Almond Extract
- 1 Cup Vegetable Oil
- 2 1/2 Cups All Purpose Flour
- 1 3/4 teaspoons Baking Powder
- 1/2 teaspoon Baking Soda
- 1 teaspoon Salt

ORANGE SIMPLE SYRUP

- 2 Oranges, just the peels
- 3 Tablespoons Fresh Orange Juice
- 1/2 Cup Water
- 1/2 Cup Granulated Sugar

ORANGE GLAZE

- 1 Tablespoon Butter, softened
- 1 1/4 Cups Powdered Sugar
- 2 Tablespoons Heavy Cream
- 1 Tablespoon Orange Zest
- 1-2 Tablespoons Orange Juice
- 1/4 teaspoon Vanilla

INSTRUCTIONS

For the Cake

1. In a bowl, rub the sugar and zest together in your fingers until fragrant.
   - 1 1/4 Cup Sugar,2 Tablespoons Orange Zest
2. In a large bowl, or standing mixer, add orange juice, eggs, vanilla, almond extract, sugar with zest and oil. Mix for 3-4 minutes until pale in color.
   - 1 Cup Fresh Orange Juice,3 Large Eggs,1 1/2 teaspoon Vanilla,1/4 teaspoon Almond Extract,1 Cup Vegetable Oil
3. Sift in flour, salt, baking powder, baking soda and salt. Mix well until combined but do not over mix.
   - 2 1/2 Cups All Purpose Flour,1 3/4 teaspoons Baking Powder,1/2 teaspoon Baking Soda,1 teaspoon Salt
4. Spray a bundt pan with baker's spray or use nonstick spray and flour, turning the pan to coat and dumping out excess. Pour batter in the bundt pan.
5. Bake at 350 for 50-60 minutes. Remove once a toothpick comes out clean. While the cake is baking, prepare the syrup.

For the Syrup

1. Add all the ingredients to a small saucepan over medium low heat.
   - 2 Oranges,3 Tablespoons Fresh Orange Juice,1/2 Cup Water,1/2 Cup Granulated Sugar
2. Bring to a simmer, stirring occasionally until the sugar is totally dissolved. Set aside until cake is done baking.
3. When the cake is done, remove it from the oven and while it is still warm, prick the cake all over with a skewer and then pour over the syrup. Allow to cool 30 minutes in the pan before turning out onto a cooling rack and wait for it to cool completely.

For the Glaze

1. Add all the ingredients to the bowl of a stand mixer and using the whisk attachment, mix until well combined and smooth.
   - 1 Tablespoon Butter,1 1/4 Cups Powdered Sugar,2 Tablespoons Heavy Cream,1 Tablespoon Orange Zest,1-2 Tablespoons Orange Juice,1/4 teaspoon Vanilla
2. Place a piece of parchment paper next to the cooling rack. Transfer the cooling rack with the cake to the clean paper and pour the glaze onto the top of the cake.
3. Allow it to sit then place another piece of paper or silpat next to the cake and move it to the clean sheet.
4. Pour the remaining glaze from the parchment onto the cake. You may have to repeat this step a few times until you have as much of the glaze as possible on the cake.

Dennis Rader (BTK)

Dennis Lynn Rader (born March 9, 1945), also known as BTK (an abbreviation he gave himself for "bind, torture, kill"), is an American serial killer who murdered at least ten people in Wichita and Park City, Kansas, between 1974 and 1991. Although Rader occasionally killed or attempted to kill men and children, he typically targeted women. His victims were often bound, sometimes with objects from their homes, and either suffocated with a plastic bag or manually strangled with a ligature.

In addition, Rader stole keepsakes from his female victims, including underwear, licenses, and personal items. He often sent taunting letters to police and media outlets, describing the details of his crimes. In 2004, after a 13-year hiatus, Rader resumed sending letters, leading to his 2005 arrest and subsequent guilty plea. He is currently serving ten consecutive life sentences at the El Dorado Correctional Facility.

STUFFED AND TIED PORK LOIN

BOUND, TIED AND STUFFED LOIN

INGREDIENTS

Units USMScale1x2x3x

- *1 (3 1/2- to 4 lb.) boneless pork loin roast*
- *1 cup panko*
- *1/2 cup grated Parmesan cheese*
- *4 Tbsp. unsalted butter, melted*
- *2 Tbsp. dried herb blend (Italian herb blend, herb de Provence, or make your own)*
- *1 1/2 tsp. salt, divided*
- *1 1/2 tsp. pepper, divided*
- *About 5 ribs celery (optional)*

INSTRUCTIONS

1. *Preheat the oven to 350°F.*
2. *Meanwhile, place the pork on a cutting board, fat side down. With a sharp boning or carving knife, cut down along one long side of the loin, about ½ inch from the edge, stopping ½ inch from the cutting board. Turn the knife parallel to the cutting board and cut inward ½ inch above the cutting board, unrolling the roast like a carpet. Continue until the loin is one long flat piece, about ½ inch thick.*
3. *Mix together the panko, cheese, butter, herbs, 1 teaspoon salt, and 1 teaspoon pepper. Spread the mixture all over the pork. Beginning at the end that was the*

interior, roll the roast up and tie with kitchen twine every 1 ½ to 2 inches. Sprinkle with the remaining ½ teaspoon salt and ½ teaspoon pepper.

4. *Put the pork on a rack in a roasting pan fat side up. If you don't have a rack use about 5 stalks of celery arranged in the pan.*
5. *Roast until the internal temperature is 145-160°F, 20 to 25 minutes per pound. 145°F is considered safe for pork according to the USDA. It will be moist and slightly pink in the center. If you prefer your pork fully white and well done, then go with the 160°F temperature.*
6. *Cover the roasting pan with foil and let rest for 30 minutes.*
7. *Meanwhile, increase the oven to 475°F.*
8. *Roast uncovered for another 10 minutes, until the meat is nicely browned.*
9. *Remove the twine, slice the roast, and serve immediately.*

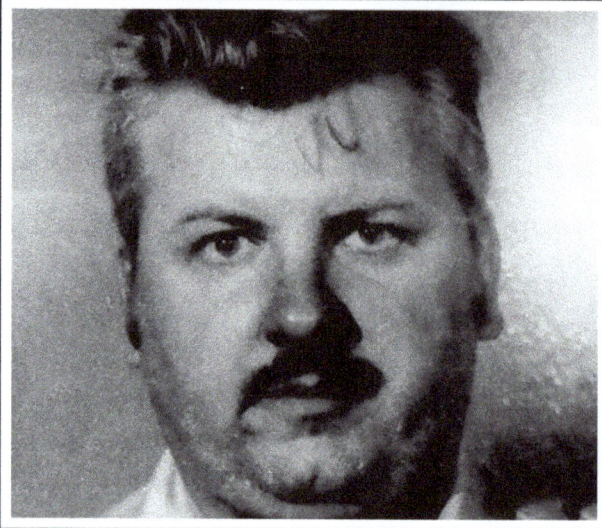

John Wayne Gacy

Gacy committed his first known murder in January 1972, after luring the 16-year-old Timothy McCoy to his house for sex. The next morning, Gacy saw McCoy standing in the bedroom doorway with a knife and rushed to attack him, wrestling the knife away and stabbing McCoy to death. Afterward, Gacy belatedly realized that McCoy hadn't been attacking or threatening Gacy but rather was holding the knife because he had just made them breakfast. Nevertheless, Gacy discovered he received sexual gratification from killing McCoy.

Gacy pleaded not guilty by reason of insanity, and he went to trial on 33 murder charges. The prosecution argued Gacy was sane and in control of his actions, pointing to the elaborate steps Gacy took to both prepare for and conceal his murders. "These were certainly the acts of a man capable of premeditation, acting in his own best interest under duress, and recollecting the details of his criminal activities," said chief prosecutor William Kunkle, according to Killer Clown. Mental health professionals testified for both sides about Gacy's mental state.

COTTON CANDY CAKE POPS

ODE TO JOHN WAYNE GACY

PLAY WITH THE SWEET CLOWN POPS

FOR THE VANILLA CAKE

- 4 large eggs
- ½ cup (125 ml) granulated sugar
- 2 tbsp. (30 ml) vegetable oil or melted butter
- 1 tsp. (5 ml) vanilla extract
- 1 cup (250 ml) all-purpose flour
- ½ tsp. (2 ml) baking powder

FOR THE VANILLA FROSTING (SEE NOTE)

- 1/3 cup (80 ml) butter, room temperature
- 1 ¼ cups (310 ml) powdered sugar
- ½ tsp. (2 ml) vanilla extract
- 1 tbsp. (15 ml) milk (if needed)

TO ASSEMBLE THE CAKE POPS

- Lollipop sticks
- 1 little (215 g) Chocolats Favoris Cotton Candy fondue
- Cake sprinkles (optional)

INSTRUCTIONS

- *Makes about 18 cake pops.*

FOR THE VANILLA CAKE

- *Preheat the oven to 350°F (175°C). Grease and lightly flour an 8-in (20 cm) round cake pan.*
- *In a large bowl, beat the eggs and sugar until the mixture is pale yellow and light. Mix in the oil or melted butter and the vanilla extract. In a small bowl, whisk the flour and baking powder together. Then, add to the liquid ingredients. Mix to fully incorporate (make sure there are no lumps).*
- *Pour the cake batter into the prepared pan. Bake for 20 minutes (or until the cake is puffed up and golden brown).*
- *Let the cake cool completely. Unmold, wrap in plastic wrap, and refrigerate until ready to assemble the cake pops.*

FOR THE VANILLA FROSTING

- *In a large bowl, beat the butter until it's smooth and creamy. Sift the powdered sugar, then add to the butter and mix at low speed to incorporate.*
- *Add the vanilla extract and beat at high speed until the frosting is creamy and fluffy.*
- *Add the milk if the frosting seems too thick and beat at high speed to fully incorporate it.*

TO ASSEMBLE THE CAKE POPS

- *Slice the cake in halves. Break one half of the cake into crumbs, putting the crumbs in a measuring cup as you go. You need about 4 cups (1 L) of cake crumbs for this recipe (wrap the remaining cake half and freeze for a future batch).*
- *Transfer the cake crumbs to the bowl that contains the frosting. Using a spatula, mix the cake crumbs into the frosting and pressing the mixture onto the sides of the bowl to thoroughly incorporate. The cake crumbs should be fully coated with icing, but the mixture should be just wet enough for it to stick together when firmly pressed. If the combination seems too wet, mix in additional cake crumbs until you reach the right texture.*
- *Portion the mixture into 2 tbsp. (30 ml) balls and roll firmly between your palms. Set the cake pop balls on a clean baking sheet as you go. Once you've rolled all the cakes, transfer the baking sheet to the freezer for 30 minutes to harden.*
- *While the cake pop balls cool, bring a pot of water to the boil and prepare the Cotton Candy fondue according to the packaging instructions.*
- *Remove the fondue can from the boiling water and pat dry. Open the can and stir the fondue to make it super smooth. Take the cake pop balls out of the freezer. Dip the tip of a lollipop stick into the fondue, then stick it into a cake pop ball,*

inserting it deep into the ball. Return this cake pop to the baking sheet and repeat to create all cake pops. Return the treats to the freezer for 5 minutes to make sure the sticks are solid.

- One after the other, dip the cake pops into the Cotton Candy fondue to fully coat them with the fondue. Garnish with sprinkles, if desired. Stick the cake pops in a cardboard box or a foam brick and let rest for about 20 minutes to set (you can speed up this process by refrigerating the cake pops).
- Enjoy the cake pops right away or store them in the refrigerator until ready to serve

Zodiac

"I like killing people because it's so much fun."

In July of 1969, a letter arrived at *The San Francisco Examiner* newspaper containing those chilling words in a coded message. The sender: the soon-to-be-notorious Zodiac, a serial killer who terrorized Northern California in the late 1960s and early 1970s with a combination of grisly murders and bizarre public letters brimming with horrific threats, demented demands and mysterious ciphers teasing his identity.

That identity has stymied law-enforcement officials, professional code breakers and armchair criminologists alike for nearly five decades. While officially connected to five murders and two attempted murders, the Zodiac hinted he had killed at least 37 victims. After taunting the police and the public with nearly two dozen communiqués, he seemed to vanish in the late 1970s. But his twisted legacy endures, having inspired three real-life copycat killers and dozens of books, TV shows and movies—including, most famously, Clint Eastwood's nemesis in the film "Dirty Harry."

ZEN TABOULAH SALAD

CAN YOU SOLVE IT SALAD?

INGREDIENTS

- 2 cups water
- 1 cup quinoa
- 1 pinch salt
- ¼ cup olive oil
- ½ teaspoon sea salt
- ¼ cup lemon juice
- 3 tomatoes, diced
- 1 cucumber, diced
- 2 bunches green onions, diced
- 2 carrots, grated
- 2 stalks celery, diced
- 1 cup chopped fresh parsley

DIRECTIONS

1. Bring water to a boil in a medium saucepan; add quinoa and a pinch of salt. Reduce heat to low, cover and simmer for 15 minutes. Allow to cool to room temperature; fluff with a fork.
2. Meanwhile, combine olive oil, sea salt, lemon juice, tomatoes, cucumber, green onions, carrots, and parsley in a large bowl; stir in cooled quinoa. Refrigerate for 2 hours and serve

The Night Stalker

Theft turned to violence with Ramirez's first discovered murder on June 28, 1984; the victim was 79-year-old Jennie Vincow, who was sexually assaulted, stabbed, and killed during a burglary in her home. What followed was a spree of brutal murders, rapes, and robberies, leaving dozens of victims in his wake.

Ramirez next struck nearly nine months later. On March 17, 1985, he attacked Maria Hernandez, who managed to escape, and then killed her roommate, Dayle Okazaki, 34. Not satisfied with these assaults, he also shot and killed Tsai-Lian Yu, 30, the same evening, spurring a media frenzy that saw Ramirez dubbed the "Valley Intruder" by the press.

A full-scale police operation yielded no concrete results, and Ramirez repeated his attack pattern on retirees William and Lillian Doi in May 1985. Over the next few months, his murder rate escalated, claiming another dozen victims in a frenzy of burglary, assault, and brutal violence, complete with Satanic rituals. The Los Angeles Police Department responded by putting together a dedicated task force, with the FBI stepping in to assist.

Ramirez's actions on his final night of terror—August 24, 1985, in the Los Angeles area—soon led to his capture. First, he was spotted outside a Mission Viejo home, where he unwittingly left a footprint, before the witness took note of his car and license plate. Later, after Ramirez raped another woman at her home (and shot her fiancé), the victim provided a detailed description of her assailant, who had forced her to swear her love for Satan.

BEEF ENCHILADAS

ODE TO RICHARD RAMIREZ

SATAN'S ENCHILADAS

INGREDIENTS

11/2 lb. ground beef 80/20
1 small onion diced
1 teaspoon of cumin
1 teaspoon of chili powder
1 teaspoon of garlic powder
½ cup of taco sauce (Taco bell, mild, medium or hot
1 ½ cups grated cheese (sharp cheddar or Jalapeno Jack)
1 dozen corn tortillas
1 cup vegetable oil

Brown ground beef with onion and drain off grease. Add spices with taco sauce. Bring to a simmer and add ¼ cup of water. Leave on low. Heat oil and cook tortillas to only a soft cook, Drain on a paper towel. In a 9s13 pan one tortilla at a time, fill with ground beef mixture and roll. Cover with enchilada sauce and cheese. Cover with aluminum foil and bake for 45 minutes at 350. Let rest for 5-10 minutes.

ENCHILADA SAUCE

- 3 tablespoons avocado oil
- 3 tablespoons all-purpose flour
- 2 to 3 tablespoons chili powder, to taste
- ½ teaspoon ground cumin
- ½ teaspoon garlic powder
- ½ teaspoon sea salt
- ¼ teaspoon dried oregano
- 1 (8-ounce) can tomato sauce
- 1½ cups vegetable broth

INSTRUCTIONS

1. Heat the avocado oil in a small saucepan over medium heat. Add the flour and whisk for 1 minute. Add the chili powder, cumin, garlic powder, salt, and oregano and whisk for 1 minute. Slowly add the tomato sauce and then the broth, whisking continuously until smooth.
2. Simmer for 12 minutes, or until thickened. The sauce will thicken more as it cools. Use in your favorite enchilada recipe.
3. Makes 1¾ cups.

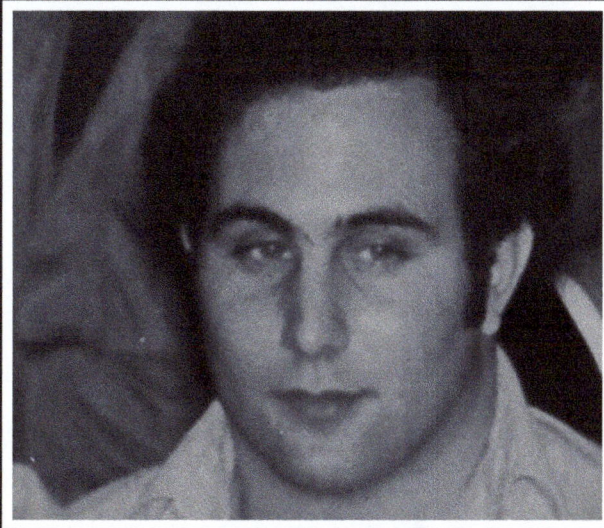

Son of Sam

The shootings first attributed to the killer who would become known as the Son of Sam occurred in the Pelham Bay area of the Bronx. Two women, Jody Valenti and Donna Lauria, 18, were sitting in Valenti's double-parked Oldsmobile when a man approached the car and fired three bullets. Lauria was killed instantly and Valenti was shot in the thigh before the man walked quickly away. Valenti described her attacker as a white male in his thirties, approximately 5-foot-8 and about 200 pounds, with short, dark, curly hair.

In the early hours of the morning, Valentina Suriani, 18, and her boyfriend, Alexander Esau, 20, were sitting in Suriani's car near her home in the Bronx when they were each shot twice. Esau died at the scene and Suriani later in hospital. For the first time, the killer announced his identity via a handwritten note left for police at the crime scene in which he referred to himself as "Son of Sam" and promised the killings would continue.

Berkowitz, 24, of Yonkers, N.Y. was arrested in front of his apartment building. Police had investigated Berkowitz's car and discovered a rifle in the back seat, maps of the crime scenes and ammunition. Waiting until Berkowitz left the apartment building, police arrested him as he sat behind the wheel of his car. A bag containing the .44 caliber revolver was recovered next to him, and a smiling Berkowitz reportedly said to the arresting officer, "Well, you got me."

The following day Berkowitz would confess to the shootings, claiming that Sam was a demonic spirit who spoke to him via his former neighbor's black Labrador. Berkowitz also told police he was responsible for 1,500 fires set around the city. He was 23 at the time of the first murder.

CHICKEN AND NOODLES

CHICKEN AND NOODLES YADA YADA

2 teaspoons onion powder
1 (26 ounce) can condensed cream of chicken soup
1 (10.75 ounce) can condensed cream of mushroom soup
2 cups diced, cooked chicken breast
1 large carrot diced
1 large celery stalk diced
¼ small sweet onion diced
1 teaspoon seasoning salt
½ teaspoon garlic powder
11/2 Tablespoons Chicken Boullion
2 (9 ounce) packages frozen egg noodles

DIRECTIONS

1. Gather the ingredients.
2. Saute' carrot, celery and onion in butter until softened, onions are semi clear. Add the next ingredients
3. Combine chicken broth, both condensed soups, and diced chicken in a large pot. Season with onion powder, seasoning salt, and garlic powder.
4. Bring to a boil over high heat and stir in noodles.

Manson Family

Manson was influenced not only by drugs, but also by art works and music of the time, most notably The Beatles song "Helter Skelter" from their 1968 *White Album*. *Helter Skelter: The True Story of the Manson Murders* was later the title of a best-selling book about Manson and his crimes.

Paul McCartney has said that the playground slide in "Helter Skelter" was a metaphor for the rise and fall of the Roman Empire. Manson, however, interpreted the song's lyrics as incitation to begin a race war. He turned to the album and lyrics to justify his scheme and guide his followers to murder.

Manson had a strong belief and interest in the notion of Armageddon from the Book of Revelations and also explored the teachings of Scientology and more obscure cult churches, such as the Church of the Final Judgment.

In many ways, Manson reflected personality traits and obsessions that were associated with gurus of cult-quasi-religious groups that began to emerge in the 1960s. He was pathologically deluded into believing that he was the harbinger of doom regarding the planet's future.

The Manson Family—including Manson and his young, loyal disciples—is thought to have carried out some 35 murders. Most of their cases were never tried, in part for lack of evidence. The perpetrators had also already been sentenced to life for brutally killing seven people—actor Sharon Tate and wealthy supermarket executive Leno LaBianca and his wife, Rosemary, among them—on back-to-back nights in August 1969.

HERB CRUSTED CHICKEN BREAST

ODE TO THE MANSON FAMILY KILLERS

MANSON'S FAVORITE BOOBS

INGREDIENTS

2 boneless skinless chicken breasts (5–8 oz. each) fork pricked on both sides
1 cup Italian Salad Dressing
1/2 cup panko Italian breadcrumbs
1/4 cup Parmesan, grated
2 teaspoons Italian seasoning
1/2 teaspoon dried sage
Salt and pepper to taste

INSTRUCTIONS

1. Marinate the chicken in the Italian Dressing for 20 minutes dredge the chicken breasts in the panko mixture, patting it in to adhere until fully coated.
2. Combine breadcrumbs, Parmesan, Italian seasoning, sage and salt and pepper to taste to make the breading. Dredge the chicken breasts in the panko mixture, patting it in to adhere until fully coated
3. Transfer chicken to a baking sheet and bake at 425°F for about 20 minutes or until the chicken is cooked through and the crust has browned.

Peter Clemenza

Clemenza became a friend of Vito Corleone after Vito immigrated from Sicily to the United States as well. As a young man, Vito held a blanket of guns for him to prevent their discovery by the police. Clemenza repaid this favor by stealing a crimson rug for Vito's family, with the unwitting Vito's help, thus facilitating the future godfather's first introduction to the rewards of crime, like theft. Their roles were later reversed when Vito killed Don Fanucci, establishing him as the group's leader as he had the charisma Fatty Clemenza lacked. Friendly and jovial, Clemenza was known as a storyteller among many of his acquaintances, friends and family members - a trait that endeared him to Vito, who loved listening to storytellers, even if the stories were all made up or mythology. Peter Clemenza got his start selling stolen goods such as dresses, wine, chocolate and guns with Vito and Tessio as far back as 1917, and became a key figure in the growing Corleone family. Vito kept him close through the years - even making him godfather to his oldest son Santino - though this was all to control his brutal and more ambitious tendencies, as Sonny always had a temper.

When Paulie Gatto was discovered as the true traitor, Clemenza was entrusted with the task of eliminating him, enlisting rising associate Rocco Lampone to carry out the hit. Clemenza took Paulie's betrayal personally, having shepherded Paulie's rise through the family over the heads of more experienced and loyal soldiers In order to lull Paulie into a false sense of security, Clemenza and Rocco drove around in a car with him for a few hours, looking for good sites where the Corleone men could «go to the mattresses» in the imminent war. He also collected some cannoli for his wife at The Albatross Grill. After this, Clemenza ordered Paulie to pull the car over at some railyards in Brooklyn so he could take a piss. While Clemenza was urinating on the ground, Rocco shot Paulie in the back of the head three times while Clemenza finished. Rocco succeeded Paulie as a button man and Don Corleone's new driver before becoming a Soldato.

CANOLLI

LEAVE THE GUN, TAKE THE CANOLLI

2 cups all-purpose flour
2 tablespoons granulated sugar
3 tablespoons unsalted butter
¼ teaspoon kosher salt
⅓ cup marsala wine
1 large egg
1 egg yolk, set aside egg white for brushing

FILLING

16 ounces ricotta cheese, strained (Strain for 2-3 hours)
½ cup powdered sugar
1 teaspoon vanilla extract

INSTRUCTIONS

1. *Add the flour, sugar, and salt to the food processor and pulse until just combined. Then add in the cold butter and pulse until you have small crumbles. You can also make the dough by hand the same way you would make pie crust.*
2. *Add the whole egg, egg yolk, and marsala and pulse until the dough comes together into a shaggy ball.*
3. *Turn the dough out onto a clean surface and knead for 2-4 minutes until you have a smooth ball. Place the dough in a lightly oiled bowl, cover, and rest for 1 hour.*

4. *While the dough is resting, add about 2 inches of vegetable oil to a large pot or Dutch oven over medium heat until it reaches 350°F.*
5. *Roll out the dough as thin as possible (⅛th to 1/16ᵗʰ inch thick) and use a 4 inch cookie cutter to cut into rounds. For mini cannoli use a 2 inch cookie cutter.*
6. *Lightly brush the cannoli forms with vegetable oil and then wrap the cannoli dough around each form. Brush the edge where the ends meet with egg white and press gently to seal.*
7. *Fry the shells at 350°F for about 1 minute on each side until golden brown and crispy. Only fry 4-5 at a time so as not to crowd the pan.*
8. *Use tongs to transfer the cannoli to a paper towel to drain. Immediately remove the form from the cannoli (you can use the tongs and a paper towel to gently wiggle it off the form, just be careful!).*
9. *Let the forms cool fully and repeat the process with the remaining dough circles. Let the cannoli shells cool fully before filling.*
10. *While the cannoli are cooling, make the filling.*
11. *Add the strained ricotta, powdered sugar, and vanilla to a large bowl. Using a hand mixer, whip the ricotta until it's fully combined and smooth. If desired, fold in chopped nuts or chocolate chips!*
12. *When ready to use transfer to a piping bag, snip the tip off and fill the shells. Then press on desired toppings!*
13. *Top of Form*
14. *Bottom of Form*

Jack the Ripper

Jack the Ripper terrorized London in 1888, killing at least five women and mutilating their bodies in an unusual manner, indicating that the killer had a substantial knowledge of human anatomy. The culprit was never captured—or even identified—and Jack the Ripper remains one of England's, and the world's, most infamous criminals.

All five killings attributed to Jack the Ripper took place within a mile of each other, in or near the Whitechapel district of London's East End, from August 7 to September 10, 1888. Several other murders occurring around that time period have also been investigated as the work of "Leather Apron" (another nickname given to the murderer).

A number of letters were allegedly sent by the killer to the London Metropolitan Police Service (often known as Scotland Yard), taunting officers about his gruesome activities and speculating on murders to come. The moniker "Jack the Ripper" originates from a letter—which may have been a hoax—published at the time of the attacks.

Jack the Ripper's murders suddenly stopped in the fall of 1888, but London citizens continued to demand answers that would not come, even more than a century later. The ongoing case—which has spawned an industry of books, films, TV series and historical tours—has met with a number of hindrances, including lack of evidence, a gamut of misinformation and false testimony, and tight regulations by Scotland Yard.

Jack the Ripper didn't just snuff out life with a knife, he mutilated and disemboweled women, removing organs such as kidneys and uteruses, and his crimes seemed to portray an abhorrence for the entire female gender.

PULLED PORK

RIPPED OFF THE BUTT BONE

This can be made in a slow cooker, InstaPot or on a smoker

4 lb pork shoulder, or butt
Mix dry ingredients
2 Tablespoons oil (optional if searing)
1 Tbsp brown sugar
1 tablespoon chili powder
1 teaspoon onion powder
1 teaspoon garlic powder
1 teaspoon cumin
1 teaspoon kosher salt
1 teaspoon black pepper
½ teaspoon smoked hickory salt
1 teaspoon ground mustard

Mix all dry ingredients. Then place on meat and rub into the meat. Let stand for 30 minutes. Place in pan or over, this can also be cooked in a slow cooker, oven or smoker. ½ cup to a cup of water in the bottom of the pan and cover with foil. Set at 350 degrees. Check every hour for moisture and add water as needed. It will take approximately 4-5 hours.

*If smoked, smoke to 145, put in aluminum pan and wrap with foil and cook to 205. Pull off and rest for approximately 1 hour uncovered.

III.
KINKERY

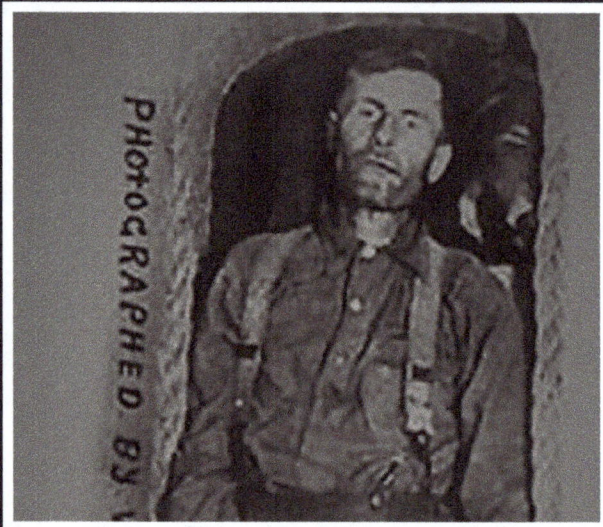

Elmer McCurdy

The bizarre tale of Elmer's journey from varmint to traveling corpse started in Oklahoma when he and his gang of bandits robbed the wrong train in October 1911. The crew made off with a paltry $45 and a load of whiskey. A posse closed in on the outlaw two days later and McCurdy swore he'd never be taken alive! Living up to his word, he died after an hour long shootout and was later identified as one of the five bandits that had robbed a train in Coffeyville, KS earlier that year.

His body was taken to the Johnson Funeral Home in Pawhuska, OK, where it was embalmed. After it sat unclaimed at the mortuary for six months, one observer noticed Elmer was perfectly preserved. Attempting to cash-in on a growing local interest in the "Embalmed Bandit," the enterprising mortician dressed Elmer up with rifle in hand and put him on display for five cents per view.

In 1916, two carnival promoters posing as McCurdy's brothers claimed the corpse. Afterwards, Elmer traveled across the country with the Great Patterson Carnival Show as an attraction in a sideshow of human curiosities.

Louis Sonney, head of an entertainment company in California, acquired Elmer in 1922 after a carny used the body as a security deposit and then defaulted on a $500 loan. Sonney put the mummified bandit in his travelling show, the Museum of Crime, which toured up and down the West Coast up until the 1940s.

BBQ WEENIES AND MEATBALLS

ODE TO ELMER MCCURDY

MCCURDY ENCASED MEATS

1 large package of little smokies
1 package of regular meatballs
1 12 ounce bottle of BBQ sauce
1 12 ounce bottle of grape jelly

Brown little smokies and add meatballs put in a crock pot or aluminum pan to cook in the smoker. Add the BBQ sauce and jelly, mix together. Cover with foil and put on the smoker or turn on the crock pot to high. Cook for 2-3 hours, 165 temp.

Mae West

In 1926, West got her first starring role in a Broadway play entitled *Sex*, which she wrote, produced, and directed. Though the play was a hit at the box office, the "more respectable" Broadway critics panned it for its explicit sexual content. The production also did not go over well with city officials, who raided the show and arrested West along with much of the cast. She was prosecuted on morals charges and on April 19, 1927, sentenced to 10 days in jail on Welfare Island (now known as Roosevelt Island) in New York. The incarceration was cordial, as West reportedly dined with the warden and his wife on a few occasions. She served eight days, with two off for good behavior. The media attention of the entire affair did nothing but enhance her career.

The blunt sexuality and steamy settings of her films aroused the wrath and moral indignation of several groups. One of these was the Motion Picture Production Code, also known as the Hays Code for its creator, Will H. Hays. The organization had the power to pre-approve films' productions and change scripts. On July 1, 1934, the organization began to seriously and meticulously enforce the code on West's screenplays, and heavily edited them. West responded in her typical fashion by increasing the number of innuendos and double entendres, fully expecting to confuse the censors, which she did for the most part.

- *It is better to be looked over than overlooked.*
- *Between two evils, I always pick the one I never tried before.*
- *There are no good girls gone wrong—just bad girls found out.*

TWICE BAKED POTATOES

DON'T JUST MAKE IT ONCE, WHEN YOU CAN MAKE IT TWICE

4 large baking potatoes
8 slices bacon
1 cup sour cream
½ cup milk
4 tablespoons butter
½ teaspoon salt
½ teaspoon pepper
½ teaspoon smoked paprika
½ teaspoon ground mustard
½ teaspoon garlic powder
1 cup shredded Cheddar cheese, divided
8 green onions, sliced, divided

DIRECTIONS

1. *Gather ingredients and preheat the oven to 350 degrees F (175 degrees C).*
2. *Bake potatoes in the preheated oven until tender, about 1 hour, depending on the size of your potatoes. Set potatoes aside until cool enough to handle.*
3. *Meanwhile, place bacon in a large, deep skillet. Cook over medium-high heat until evenly brown. Drain, crumble, and set aside.*
4. *Slice potatoes in half lengthwise and scoop the flesh into a large bowl; save skins.*
5. *Add sour cream, milk, butter, salt, pepper, 1/2 cup cheese, and 1/2 of the green onions to the potato; mix with a hand mixer until well blended and creamy.*
6. *Spoon the mixture into the potato skins; top each with remaining cheese, green onions, and bacon.*
7. *Return potatoes to the preheated oven and continue baking until the cheese is melted, about 15 minutes. Serve Hot!*

Christian Gray

Christian was born in the city of Detroit. His biological mother, Ella, was addicted to drugs and worked as a prostitute. Her pimp was extremely abusive to both her and Christian, often beating Cristian with a belt, hitting and kicking him, or putting out his cigarettes on his skin, leaving terrible scars and burn marks. When he was four years old, his mother overdosed and died; he was alone with her corpse for four days before they were discovered by police.

Christian continues to have nightmares of his childhood even well into adulthood, and often calls his biological mother "the crack whore." Dr. Grace Trevelyan Grey was the emergency room doctor on staff when the traumatized Christian was brought to the hospital by the police. She and her husband, Carrick Grey, adopted Christian into their family, but while they were waiting for the adoption paperwork to go through, he lived with a foster family for several months, which included a ten year old Jack Hyde.

As an adolescent, Christian had violent mood swings that often got him into fights, and he secretly drank and was addicted to alcohol. He hated all of the therapists that he was forced to meet with, because none of them were helping him. When he was fifteen years old, he took a landscaping job for his mother's friend Elena Lincoln.

Elena seduced him, and he ended up losing his virginity to her. She introduced him to the BDSM lifestyle, which he credits with teaching him how to control his emotions and channel his anger into positive outlets. She acted as a Domme to Christian for six years, until Elena's then-husband found out, and beat her to the point that she was hospitalized.

WHIPPED PINEAPPLE CREAM

SUBMISSION PINEAPPLE CREAM

1 pound frozen pineapple
1 1/4 cups almond milk (or orange juice)
1 sprig of fresh mint
1 tablespoon honey (optional) *use Maple Syrup for a vegan dessert.

Combine ingredients in a blender of smoothie machine and pulsate until desired consistency. Place in a ziplock bag, snip the corner and pipe into a glass. Add mint for garnish.

Betty Paige

Bettie Mae Page (April 22, 1923 – December 11, 2008) was an American model who gained notoriety in the 1950s for her pin-up photos. She was often referred to as the "Queen of Pinups": her long jet-black hair, blue eyes, and trademark bangs have influenced artists for generations. After her death, *Playboy* founder Hugh Hefner called her «a remarkable lady, an iconic figure in pop culture who influenced sexuality, taste in fashion, someone who had a tremendous impact on our society».

From late 1951 or early 1952 through 1957, she posed for photographer Irving Klaw for mail-order photographs with pin-up and BDSM themes, making her the first famous bondage model. Klaw also used Page in several short, black-and-white 8mm and 16mm «specialty» films, which catered to specific requests from his clientele. These silent one-reel featurettes showed women clad in lingerie and high heels, acting out fetishistic scenarios of abduction, domination, and slave-training; bondage, spanking, and elaborate leather costumes and restraints were included periodically. Page alternated between playing a stern dominatrix, and a helpless victim bound hand and foot.

The reasons reported for Page's departure from modeling vary. Some reports[which?] mention the Kefauver Hearings of the United States Senate Special Committee to Investigate Crime in Interstate Commerce as a potential reason, after a young man apparently died during a session of bondage which was rumored to be inspired by images featuring Page. After leaving modeling, Page converted to Christianity and became a born again evangelist on December 31, 1959, while living in Key West, Florida. She recalled in 1998, "When I gave my life to the Lord, I began to think he disapproved of all those nude pictures of me."

BEEF TIPS AND NOODLES

TASTIEST LEATHER AND LACE

- 1 (10.5 ounce) can condensed cream of mushroom soup
- 1 (1.25 ounce) package beef with onion soup mix
- 1 medium onion diced
- 1 carrot diced
- 1 (4.5 ounce) can mushrooms, drained
- 1 cup water
- 1 pound sirloin tips, cubed
- 1 (16 ounce) package wide egg noodles

DIRECTIONS

1. Gather the ingredients. Preheat the oven to 400 degrees F (200 degrees C).
2. Combine condensed soup, soup mix, mushrooms,carrots onions and water in a 13x9-inch casserole dish. Mix thoroughly and add beef tips. Turn to coat well. Bake in the preheated oven for 1 hour.
3. While beef tips are cooking, bring a large pot of lightly salted water to a boil. Add noodles and cook for 8 to 10 minutes or until al dente; drain.
4. Serve Beef tips over noodles

Jessica Rabbit

She attests to Eddie Valiant that «I›m not bad, I›m just drawn that way». Indeed, she proves herself to be selfless and compassionate throughout the movie. Although she seems cool and distant, she has a soft spot for Roger, whom she married because he «makes her laugh», is a better lover than a driver, and that he›s magnificent and «better than Goofy". She calls him her "honey bunny" and "darling". She adores him beyond measure and is irrefutably loyal to him. As proof of her love, she tells Eddie that she'll pay any price for Roger and helps prove Roger innocent by assisting with the investigation.

She makes it clear that despite what others think of her, she only has eyes for Roger and would do anything for his sake. She proves to be brave, quick-witted, and intuitive; she knowingly puts herself at risk to save Roger and Eddie. Yet despite the danger, she maintains a calm composure and exhibits great skill in combat, including handling a gun. While she maintains a calm and collected demeanor, for the most part, the first time she loses her composure is when Judge Doom shows her and Eddie his deadly Dip and machine to destroy Toontown, and when she and Roger are almost sprayed by the deadly substance, she sighs in relief, but feels she might faint.

Jessica is a statuesque tall, voluptuous and gorgeous woman with a curvy and slender hourglass figure with a narrow waist and large, broad hips. She has fair skin and long, luxurious red hair with side-bangs that usually cover her right eye. Her green eyes are heavy-lidded and seductive with long dark lashes and accented by shimmering lavender eye shadow. Her nose is fairly small, especially in relation to her full, red pouting lips. Her ensemble consists of a red sequined strapless dress that reveals a lot of cleavage with a low back, sweetheart neckline, and high thigh slit.

MINI DEVIL FOOD CAKES

PATTY CAKE, PATTY CAKES

1 cup (226 g) unsalted butter
½ cup (118 ml) whole milk
1 cup (236 ml) water
¾ cup (75 g) Dutch-process cocoa powder
1 teaspoon instant coffee optional,
2 cups (250 g) all-purpose flour
1 cup (200 g) granulated sugar
1 cup (200 g) light brown sugar firmly packed
1 ½ teaspoons baking soda
1 teaspoon baking powder
1 teaspoon salt
¾ cup (190 g) sour cream
2 large eggs room temperature preferred
2 teaspoons vanilla extract

Measure flour, cocoa, baking powder, baking soda and sift together. In a separate bowl cream together eggs, brown sugar, white sugar, vanilla. Water, milk and sour cream. Slowly add to dry ingredients until completely incorporated. Pour into 2 9x12 sheet pans and bake at 350 for 25 minutes. Test and leave to cool.

Cut 2" circles with a biscuit cutter. Stack the circles with bottoms together and buttercream in between. When all the patty cakes are made, warm the buttercream just enough to make it pourable. Drizzle over the top of the cakes and allow it to run down the sides to cover the cakes. DO NOT OVER COAT! Repeat as needed.

BUTTER CREAM

½ cup unsalted butter softened
4 cups powdered sugar
4 Tablespoons milk

Cream 2 cups sugar and butter until completely blended. Slowly add more sugar until right consistency.

Marilyn Monroe

Monroe dreamt of becoming an actress like Jean Harlow and Lana Turner. When her husband was sent to the South Pacific, she began working in a munitions factory in Van Nuys, California. It was there that she was first discovered by a photographer.

By the time Dougherty returned in 1946, Monroe had a successful career as a model. That year, she signed her first movie contract. With the contract came a new name and image; she began calling herself "Marilyn Monroe" and dyed her hair blonde.

At first, Monroe wasn't initially considered to be star acting material. Her acting career didn't really take off until a few years later. With her breathy voice and hourglass figure, she would soon become one of Hollywood's most famous actresses. She proved her skill by winning various honors and attracting large audiences to her films.

On May 19, 1962, Monroe made her now-famous performance at John F. Kennedy's birthday celebration, singing "Happy Birthday, Mr. President." Moments later, President Kennedy appeared on stage, saying, "I can now retire from politics after having had 'Happy Birthday' sung to me in such a sweet, wholesome way."

Monroe died at her Los Angeles home on August 5, 1962, at only 36 years old. An empty bottle of sleeping pills was found by her bed.

There has been some speculation over the years that she may have been murdered, but the cause of her death was officially ruled as a drug overdose.

LEMON CHIFFON CAKE

LEMON LINGERIE CAKE

2 cups all-purpose flour
3 teaspoons baking powder
1 1/2 cups granulated sugar
1 teaspoon kosher salt
7 large eggs, separated
½ cup lemon juice
1/4 cup water
1/2 cup vegetable oil
1 teaspoon vanilla extract
1 1/2 tablespoons lemon zest (approximately 3 large lemons)
1/2 teaspoon cream of tartar

FROSTING

- 1/2 cup butter, room temperature
- 3 cups powdered sugar
- 1 tablespoon lemon zest
- 1/4 cups freshly squeezed lemon juice

INSTRUCTIONS

1. **Cake**: Preheat oven to 325°F. Arrange the oven so you can bake the cake on the lowest rack. Set aside a 10- inch tube pan (Angel Food Cake pan).
2. In the bowl of your stand mixer fitted with the *paddle attachment*, sift together the flour, baking powder, sugar, and salt.

3. *In a small bowl whisk together the egg yolks, water, oil, vanilla, and lemon zest. When combined, add this into the bowl with the flour mixture. Mix on medium-low speed until combined and smooth, scraping the sides of the bowl as necessary.*

4. *Place the egg whites in a separate large mixing bowl with the cream of tartar. With the whisk attachment or a hand mixer, beat the egg whites on high speed until stiff peaks form.*

5. *Fold the egg whites into the batter using a rubber spatula until combined. Spoon the batter into the un-greased tube pan.*

6. *Place the pan on the lowest rack and bake for 50 minutes, or until golden and set. Cake will spring back when pressed lightly.*

7. *When the cake is done, immediately invert the pan. I like to place the pan on a wine bottle upside-down. This allows the pan to cool without trapping steam underneath, while not allowing the cake to deflate.*

8. *Allow the cake to cool for at least an hour.*

9. *When cooled, run a butter knife around the sides of the cake to release it from the pan. Gently lift the cake out. Run the knife under the cake to release it from the bottom cake pan. Place the cake on a platter.*

10. **Frosting:** *In the bowl of your stand mixer fitted with the paddle attachment mix together the butter, powdered sugar, lemon zest, and lemon juice. Turn the mixer up to medium speed and beat for 1-2 minutes until creamy, scraping the sides of the bowl as necessary,*

11. *Spread the frosting on the top of the cake and lightly frost the sides.*

Madame Du Barry

Following the death of Madame de Pompadour in 1764, Jeanne Bécu (known as "Mademoiselle Vaubernier") became the king's official mistress, and moved to Versailles in 1768. In spite of the best efforts of the Duke of Choiseul (Secretary of State and an ally of the king's former mistress) and the scorn poured upon her by the Dauphine Marie Antoinette, she managed to hold onto her place in the Court until the death of Louis XV.

By the time he met Madame du Barry, Louis XV was already an old man. He had outlived his son, the Dauphin Louis FerdinandLouis Ferdinand of France (1729-1765) died before his father and therefore never ruled, but he was the father of three Kings of France: Louis XVI, as well as Louis XVIII and Charles X, who reigned during the Restoration, his wife Marie Leszczyńska and his first official mistress and later close friend, Madame de Pompadour, among others. When the Duke of RichelieuLouis-François-Armand de Vignerot du Plessis (1696-1788), Duke of Richelieu and Marshal of France, godson of Louis XIV, son of the great-nephew of Cardinal de Richelieu heard about Jeanne Bécu, he sought to introduce her to Louis XV. The meeting was arranged in 1768 thanks to Le Bel, Premier Valet de la Chambre du Roi. Having been hastily married off to the Count Guillaume du Barry, in 1768 the new Countess was presented to the Court and became the official mistress of the monarch, who was bedazzled by her beauty. All this in spite of the best-laid plans of the Duke of ChoiseulÉtienne-François de Choiseul (1719-1785) was a leading minister during the reign of Louis XV, after the death of Cardinal de Fleury, without ever being named Prime Minister. He fell into disgrace in 1770 who was hoping to install his sister the Duchess of Grammont in this privileged position.

CREAM PUFFS

ODE TO MADAME DU BERRY

KING'S COURTESAN PUFF

PASTRY CREAM:

1 cup (236 ml) whole milk
1 cup (236 ml) heavy cream
⅓ cup (67 g) + 3 Tablespoons granulated sugar divided
1 vanilla bean[1] split in half lengthwise
¼ teaspoon salt
5 large egg yolks room temp
3 Tablespoons cornstarch
4 Tablespoons unsalted butter softened and cut into 4 pieces

CHOUX PASTRY

1 cup (236 ml) water
½ cup (113 g) unsalted butter cut into 8 pieces
¼ teaspoon salt
1 cup (125 g) all-purpose flour
4 large eggs room temperature
Powdered sugar for dusting cream puffs

INSTRUCTIONS

PASTRY CREAM (see note)

Combine cream, milk, ⅓ cup (67g) sugar, vanilla bean, and salt in a medium-sized heavy bottomed saucepan. Place on stovetop over medium heat. Stir frequently until sugar is *dissolved and mixture comes to a simmer. Remove from heat and allow to cool for 10 minutes (stir occasionally).*

- *1 cup whole milk,1 cup heavy cream,⅓ cup + 3 Tablespoons granulated sugar,1 vanilla bean[1],¼ teaspoon salt*

Meanwhile, in a separate large bowl, whisk together egg yolks and 3 Tablespoons of sugar. Whisk vigorously for about 15 seconds, until sugar is beginning to dissolve.

- *5 large egg yolks room temp*

Sprinkle cornstarch over egg/sugar mixture and whisk until combined and slightly thickened.

- *3 Tablespoons cornstarch*

Once your cream mixture has cooled, slowly drizzle about ⅓ cup of the cream mixture into the egg mixture while whisking constantly (this will temper your eggs and gradually adding the heated cream will prevent them from cooking!). Slowly, while still whisking, drizzle in the remainder of your cream mixture until the cream and egg mixture are completely combined.

Pour mixture back into saucepan and return to stovetop over medium heat. Whisk frequently until thickened.

Remove from heat and pour mixture through a fine mesh strainer into a heatproof bowl (vanilla bean should be caught by the strainer and should be discarded now).

Whisk in butter, one piece at a time until completely combined. If you didn't use a vanilla bean, stir in the vanilla extract at this point, too.

- *4 Tablespoons unsalted butter*

Place plastic wrap directly in contact with the surface of the pastry cream to keep a skin from forming. Allow to cool at room temperature for about 30 minutes or until near room temperature, then transfer to the refrigerator to chill for at least 2-4 hours. Meanwhile, prepare your choux pastry.

Moulin Rouge

In 1889, the Moulin Rouge was co-founded by Charles Zidler and Joseph Oller, who also owned the Paris Olympia. The original venue was destroyed by fire in 1915. Moulin Rouge is southwest of Montmartre, in the Paris district of Pigalle on Boulevard de Clichy in the 18th *arrondissement*, and has a landmark red windmill on its roof. The closest métro station is Blanche.

Moulin Rouge is best known as the birthplace of the modern form of the can-can dance. Originally introduced as a seductive dance by the courtesans who operated from the site, the can-can dance revue evolved into a form of entertainment of its own and led to the introduction of cabarets across Europe. Today, the Moulin Rouge is a tourist attraction, offering predominantly musical dance entertainment for visitors from around the world. The club's decor still contains much of the romance of *fin de siècle* France.

On 6 October 1889, the Moulin Rouge opened as the Jardin de Paris, an outdoor garden café-concert, at the foot of the Montmartre hill. Its creator Joseph Oller and his Manager Charles Zidler were formidable businessmen who understood the public's tastes. The aim was to attract wealthy individuals to experience the ambiance of the fashionable district of Montmartre, which was perceived as a form of slumming. The elaborate setting, featuring a garden adorned with a large elephant, provided an environment where individuals from various social strata could interact. This included workers, local residents, artists, the middle class, businessmen, stylish women, and tourists passing through Paris. Nicknamed "The First Palace of Women" by Oller and Zidler, the cabaret swiftly garnered significant acclaim.

PINK CHAMPAGNE

ODE TO MOULIN ROUGE

PINK CHAMPAGNE ROUGE

INGREDIENTS

- 2 1/4 cups all-purpose flour
- 2 1/4 tsps baking powder
- 3/4 tsp salt
- 3/4 cup unsalted butter room temperature
- 1 1/2 cup granulated sugar
- 5 large egg whites room temperature
- 1 1/2 tsp vanilla extract
- 1 cup pink champagne or sparkling wine, room temperature
- Fuschia color gel

VANILLA BUTTERCREAM:

- 5 large egg whites
- 1 1/2 cups granulated sugar
- 1 1/2 cups unsalted butter room temperature, cubed
- 1 tsp clear vanilla extract
- Fuschia color gel

ASSEMBLY:

- 2 jars of cake sparkles or 1 jar sanding sugar
- Wilton tip 1M
- Wilton tip 12

INSTRUCTIONS

PINK CHAMPAGNE CAKE:

- Preheat oven to 350F and grease and flour three 6" cake rounds, line with parchment.
- In a medium bowl, whisk flour, baking powder, and salt. Set aside.
- Using a stand mixer fitted with the paddle attachment, beat butter until smooth. Add sugar and beat on med-high until pale and fluffy (2-3mins).
- Reduce speed and add egg whites one at a time, fully incorporating after each addition. Add vanilla.
- Alternate adding flour mixture and champagne, beginning and ending with flour (3 additions of flour and 2 of champagne). Fully incorporating after each addition.
- Add a small amount of Fuschia color gel using a toothpick. Mix to incorporate but try not to overmix.
- Spread batter evenly into prepared pans. Smooth the tops with a spatula.
- Bake for approx. 35 mins or until a toothpick inserted into the center comes out mostly clean.
- Place cakes on wire rack to cool for 10mins then turn out onto wire rack to cool completely.

VANILLA BUTTERCREAM:

- Place egg whites and sugar into the bowl of a stand mixer, whisk until combined.*
- Place bowl over a hot water bath on the stove and whisk constantly until the mixture is hot and no longer grainy to the touch (approx. 3mins).
- Place bowl on your stand mixer and whisk on med-high until the meringue is stiff and cooled (the bowl is no longer warm to the touch (approx. 5-10mins)).
- Switch to paddle attachment. Slowly add cubed butter and mix until smooth. Add vanilla and continue to whip until smooth.**

ASSEMBLY:

- Place one layer of cake on a cake stand or serving plate. Top with approximately 2/3 cup of frosting and spread evenly. Repeat with remaining layers and apply a thin coat of frosting all over the cake. Chill for 20mins.
- Frost and smooth the sides. Chill for 20mins.
- Using a toothpick, add a small amount of Fuschia color gel to the remaining frosting. Stir with a spatula to incorporate, or place back on the stand mixer to mix in the color.
- Gently press cake sparkles or sanding sugar into the sides and top of the cake.***
- Decorate with pink rosettes on top and beads along the bottom if desired.

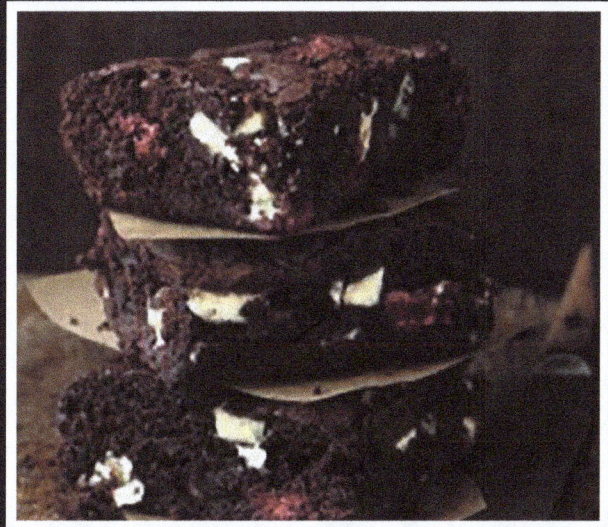

Lady Chatterly

Lady Chatterley's Lover is the final novel by English author D. H. Lawrence, which was first published privately in 1928, in Florence, Italy, and in 1929, in Paris, France. An unexpurgated edition was not published openly in the United Kingdom until 1960, when it was the subject of a watershed obscenity trial against the publisher Penguin Books, which won the case and quickly sold three million copies. The book was also banned for obscenity in the United States, Canada, Australia, India and Japan. The book soon became notorious for its story of the physical (and emotional) relationship between a working-class man and an upper-class woman, its explicit descriptions of sex and its use of then-unprintable profane words. It entered the public domain in the United States in 2024.

The contrast between mind and body can be seen in the dissatisfaction each character experiences in their previous relationships, such as Constance's lack of intimacy with her husband, who is "all mind", and Mellors's choice to live apart from his wife because of her "brutish" sexual nature. The dissatisfactions lead them into a relationship that develops very slowly and is based upon tenderness, physical passion, and mutual respect. As the relationship between Lady Chatterley and Mellors builds, they learn more about the interrelation of the mind and the body. She learns that sex is more than a shameful and disappointing act, and he learns about the spiritual challenges that come from physical love.

Lady Chatterley's Lover was banned for obscenity in the United States in 1929. In 1930, Senator Bronson Cutting proposed an amendment to the Smoot–Hawley Tariff Act, which was being debated, to end the practice of having U.S. Customs censor allegedly obscene imported books. Senator Reed Smoot vigorously opposed such an amendment and threatened to read indecent passages of imported books publicly in front of the Senate.

CHOCOLATE RASPBERRY BROWNIES

LADY CHATTERLY'S DARK SECRET

INGREDIENTS

½ cup granulated sugar
1/2 cup brown sugar
1 teaspoon vanilla extract
3 large eggs, cold
1 stick unsalted butter, roughly chopped
1 and 1/3 cup dark chocolate or semi-sweet chocolate (50-70% cocoa), broken into pieces
1 cup all-purpose flour
1/4 cup cocoa powder
Pinch of salt
1/2 fresh raspberries chopped
½ cup raspberry jam
1/2 cup chocolate chips

INSTRUCTIONS

1. *Preheat oven to 350 F. Grease and line an 8-inch square pan with baking or parchment paper, ensuring two sides overhang.*
2. *In a large mixing bowl, add sugar, brown sugar, vanilla and eggs. Whisk by hand for 30 seconds until mixture is combined and smooth.*
3. *In a separate heatproof bowl, add butter and chocolate. Heat in the microwave, stirring every 30 seconds, until melted and smooth. If it's hot to the touch, leave it for a few minutes to cool slightly.*
4. *Add chocolate mixture to the whisked eggs and sugar. Whisk by hand to combine. Then add flour, cocoa powder and salt and whisk until you have a smooth and thick brownie batter.*
5. *Fold in fresh raspberries, jam and chocolate chips. Transfer brownie batter to prepared pan and very gently smooth the top. Press a few extra raspberries into the top.*
6. *Bake brownie for about 30-35 minutes or until cooked through. It should start to crack on the edges and no longer wobble in the middle. Leave brownie in pan to cool completely before cutting into squares.*

Mata Hari

By 1904, Mata Hari rose to prominence as an exotic dancer. She was a contemporary of dancers Isadora Duncan and Ruth St. Denis, leaders in the early modern dance movement, which around the turn of the 20th century, looked to Asia and Egypt for artistic inspiration. Gabriel Astruc became her personal booking agent.

Promiscuous, flirtatious, and openly flaunting her body, Mata Hari captivated her audiences and was an overnight success from the debut of her act at the Musée Guimet on 13 March 1905. She became the long-time mistress of the millionaire industrialist Émile Étienne Guimet, who had founded the Musée. Entertainers of her era commonly invented colourful stories about their origins, and she posed as a Javanese princess of priestly Hindu birth, pretending to have been immersed in the art of sacred Indian dance since childhood. She was photographed numerous times during this period, nude or nearly so. Some of these pictures were obtained by MacLeod and strengthened his case in keeping custody of their daughter.

Mata Hari brought a carefree provocative style to the stage in her act, which garnered wide acclaim. The most celebrated segment of her act was her progressive shedding of clothing until she wore just a jeweled breastplate and some ornaments upon her arms and head. She was never seen bare-chested as she was self-conscious about having small breasts. Early in her career, she wore a bodystocking for her performances that was similar in color to her skin, but that was later omitted.

INDIAN HONEY CAKE

ODE TO MATA HARI

INDIAN DELIGHT

1 1/2 cups all-purpose flour
1 1/2 teaspoon baking powder
1/4 teaspoon salt
or 1/2 cup unsalted butter
3 eggs at room temperature
3/4 cup granulated or castor sugar
1 teaspoon vanilla extract

FOR THE HONEY SYRUP

1 cup water
1/4 cup granulated or castor sugar
6-8 tablespoons honey

FOR THE TOPPING

4 tablespoons jam
3 tablespoons desiccated coconut or dried coconut flakes

INSTRUCTIONS

TO MAKE THE CAKE :

- *Preheat your oven to 180 C / 350 F*
- *Butter and flour a 8 inch square cake pan. You can line the bottom with parchment (optional)*
- *In a bowl, whisk together flour, baking powder and salt. Keep aside.*
- *In a saucepan, heat together butter and milk until butter melts. Keep this warm until needed*
- *In a large bowl, beat together the eggs, sugar and vanilla*
- *Beat well until mixture is tripled in volume and is light and fluffy.*
- *Beat or fold in the flour mixture at low speed until all the flour is mixed in. Scrape the sides and bottom of bowl to ensure even mixing.*
- *Beat in the hot milk-butter mixture until smooth. This will take only a few seconds*
- *Pour batter immediately into prepared pan and bake for 25 to 30 minutes until top is set, springs back when pressed and maybe even lightly browned*
- *Remove from oven and cool in pan for 5 minutes.*
- *Gently remove from pan, remove parchment (if using) and cool right side up on a wire rack until cool*

TO MAKE THE HONEY SYRUP:

- *In a thick bottomed sauce pan, measure out the water and sugar*
- *Bring to a boil and then simmer for few minutes*
- *Take off heat and stir in the honey.*
- *Taste and add more honey as needed.*
- *Bring to room temperature before using.*

TO FINISH:

- *Once the cake is cool, place it right side up in serving plate or cake pan*
- *Using a skewer, poke holes in the cake all over, going till the bottom.*
- *Pour the syrup all over the cake*
- *Warm the jam a little in the microwave or over stovetop to make it easier to spread (optional)*
- *Spread jam all over the top of the cake in and smoothen*
- *Sprinkle the desiccated coconut over the top*
- *Serve immediately or ideally after resting for couple of hours at least.*

Hester Prynne

The main character of *The Scarlet Letter*, Hester Prynne, is a beautiful young woman whom readers first witness standing on the scaffolding of the town pillory. Hester is a widow who has been accused of committing adultery and having a child out of wedlock. The Puritan townspeople of Boston publicly torment and humiliate her. She holds her infant daughter, Pearl, close to her chest in an effort to conceal the letter A that has been sewn into her gown and that she must wear as a public reminder of her adulterous sins. Despite the torment Hester endures, she remains stoic and brave. Throughout the novel, she demonstrates compassion and an indomitable strength of character.

Hester primarily demonstrates her strength by refusing to name the father of her child, the minister Arthur Dimmesdale. Her character provides a stark contrast to Dimmesdale, who harbors his guilt inwardly. Hester wears the A humbly on her chest, transforming it from an object of shame and scorn to one of reverence and praise. In addition, when Hester's husband, Roger Chillingworth, returns to enact vengeance on the father of her child, Hester does not show fear. Despite the failings of both Dimmesdale to confront his guilt and Chillingworth to provide for his wife, Hester lives a fulfilling life and raises Pearl according to her own values.

CHERRY PIE

PURITAN CHERRY PIE

This recipe is enough for a double crust pie.

2 and 1/2 cups (315g) all-purpose flour (spooned & leveled), plus more for shaping and rolling
1 teaspoon salt 6 Tablespoons (85g) unsalted butter, chilled and cubed
2/3 cup (130g) vegetable shortening,
chilled 1/2 cup (120ml) ice cold water

Whisk the flour and salt together in a large bowl. 1 Add the butter and shortening. Using a pastry cutter or two forks, cut the butter and shortening into the mixture until it resembles coarse meal (pea-sized bits with a few larger bits of fat is OK). In this step, you're only breaking up the cold fat into tiny little flour-coated pieces; you're not completely incorporating it. Do not overwork the ingredients. 2 Measure 1/2 cup (120ml) of water in a cup. Add ice. Stir it around. From that, measure 1/2 cup (120ml) of water, since the ice has melted a bit. Drizzle the cold water in, 1 Tablespoon (15ml) at a time, and stir with a rubber spatula or wooden spoon after every Tablespoon has been added. Stop adding water when the dough begins to form large clumps. I always use about 1/2 cup of water, and need a little more in dry winter months. Do not add any more water than you need. 3 Transfer the pie dough to a floured work surface. Using floured hands, fold the dough into itself until the flour is fully incorporated into the fats. The dough should come together easily and should not feel overly sticky. Avoid overworking the dough. If it feels a bit too dry or crumbly, dip your fingers in the ice water and then continue bringing dough together with your hands. If it feels too sticky, sprinkle on more flour and then continue bringing dough together with your hands. Form it into a ball. Use a sharp knife to cut it in 4 Notes half. If it's helpful, you should have about 1 lb, 8 ounces dough total (about 680g). Gently flatten each half into 1-inch-thick discs using your hands. Wrap each tightly in plastic wrap. Refrigerate for at least 2 hours and up to 5 days. 5 After the dough has chilled for at least 2 hours, you can roll it out.

FILLING

4 and 1/2 cups halved & quartered pitted fresh cherries (see note)
2/3 cup (135g) granulated sugar
1/4 cup (28g) cornstarch
1 Tablespoon (15ml) lemon juice
1 teaspoon pure vanilla extract
1/4 teaspoon almond extract
11/2 teaspoon cinnamon
1 Tablespoon (14g) cold unsalted butter, cut into small cubes
egg wash: 1 large egg beaten with 1 Tablespoon (15ml) milk
optional: coarse sugar for sprinkling on crust

INSTRUCTIONS

1. *Make the filling:* In a large bowl, stir the cherries, sugar, cornstarch, lemon juice, vanilla, and almond extract together until thoroughly combined. Cover filling and place in the refrigerator as you roll out the pie dough or for up to 24 hours.
2. *Roll out the chilled pie dough:* On a floured work surface, roll out one of the discs of chilled dough (keep the *other one in the refrigerator).* Turn the dough about a quarter turn after every few rolls until you have a circle 12 inches in diameter. Carefully place the dough into a 9-inch pie dish. Tuck it in with your fingers, making sure it is smooth. Use a slotted spoon to spoon and spread the cherries into the crust. Reserve the juice for the next step. Refrigerate pie, uncovered, as you reduce the juices in the next step.
3. Pour the few Tablespoons of leftover juice into a small saucepan over low heat. Cook and stir for 3-4 minutes or until juice has slightly reduced and thickened. Cool for 5 minutes, then pour over cherries in filling. Do your best to gently toss together—doesn't have to be perfect. The reduction will harden and thicken as a result of mixing with the cold cherries. This is normal and it will melt again in the oven. Dot the pieces of butter on top of the filling.
4. Preheat oven to 400°F (204°C).
5. *Arrange the lattice:* Remove the other disc of chilled pie dough from the refrigerator. Roll the dough into a circle that is 12 inches diameter. Using a pastry wheel, sharp knife, or pizza cutter, cut strips of dough—I cut four strips 2 inches wide and two strips 1 inch wide. Carefully thread the strips over and under one another, pulling back strips as necessary to weave. Press the edges of the strips into the bottom pie crust edges to seal. Use a small paring knife to trim off excess dough. Flute or crimp the pie crust edges with a fork.
6. Lightly brush the top of the pie crust with the egg wash. Sprinkle the top with coarse sugar, if using.

7. *Place the pie onto a large baking sheet and bake for 20 minutes. Keeping the pie in the oven, turn the temperature down to 375°F (190°C) and bake for an additional 30-40 minutes or until the top crust is golden brown and the filling juices have been bubbling up around the edges or through the lattice/vents for at least 5 minutes. **After the first 20 minutes of bake time, I recommend placing a pie crust shield on the crust's edges to prevent it from over-browning too quickly.***
8. *Remove pie from the oven, place on a cooling rack, and cool for at least 3-4 hours before slicing and serving. Filling will be too juicy if the pie is warm when you slice it.*
9. *Cover leftovers tightly and store in the refrigerator for up to 5 days.*

NOTES

1. *Make Ahead / Freezing Instructions*: There are a couple ways to make this pie ahead of time. Prepare the pie in full 1 day in advance—after pie cools, cover tightly and keep at room temperature. The pie crust dough can also be prepared ahead of time and stored in the refrigerator for up to 5 days or in the freezer for up to 3 months. Baked pie also freezes well for up to 3 months. Thaw overnight in the refrigerator and allow to come to room temperature before serving. Prepared filling (with juices) can also be frozen up to 3 months, thaw overnight in the refrigerator before spooning into dough and reducing the juice.
2. *Special Tools* (affiliate links): *Cherry Pitter | Glass Mixing Bowl | Rolling Pin | Pie Dish | Pastry Wheel or Pizza Cutter | Pastry Brush | Pie Crust Shield | Cooling Rack*
3. *Cherries:* You need about 1.5 lbs of cherries for this recipe. Cut half of the cherries into halves and the remaining half of cherries into quarters. Using a mix of halved and quartered cherries helps keep the baked filling in tact. You can use any variety of cherries. I use all dark sweet cherries in the pictured pie, but also enjoy using a 50/50 combination of dark sweet and Rainier cherries. Feel free to use all Rainier cherries if desired. If using sour cherries, increase sugar to 3/4 or 1 cup depending how sweet you like your pie. You can also use frozen cherries. Halve/quarter them while they're frozen, then toss with other filling ingredients as instructed. Reduce the juices as instructed as well. Bake time may be a few minutes longer.

IV.
KULTS

Peoples Temple

Peoples Temple, religious community led by Jim Jones (1931–78) that came to international attention after some 900 of its members died at their compound, Jonestown, in Guyana, in a massive act of murder-suicide on November 18, 1978.

Jones began the Peoples Temple informally in the 1950s as an independent congregation in Indianapolis. He was inspired by the ideal of a just society that could overcome the evils of racism and poverty. Although Jones was white, he attracted mostly African Americans to the group with his vision of an integrated congregation. In 1960 the Peoples Temple affiliated with the Christian Church (Disciples of Christ), and four years later Jones was ordained. In 1965 he warned of a nuclear holocaust and led the movement to Ukiah, Calif., where members became active in both Protestant ecumenical circles and state politics. Branch congregations opened in San Francisco and Los Angeles, and the agricultural settlement Jonestown was founded in 1974.

Concerned Relatives, a group of former members, persuaded Leo J. Ryan, a U.S. congressman from California, to visit Jonestown. The visit apparently went well. However, for reasons still not completely understood, Ryan and those accompanying him were murdered when they reached the airport to return to the United States.

On November 18, 1978 one of the largest mass deaths in recorded history took place in Jonestown, Guyana. Members of the People's Temple were killed when they either drank cyanide laced Kool-Aid or if they refused they were shot by members of the security team. Among the last to drink the Kool-Aid was founder and leader Jim Jones. After everyone else was dead, including more than 300 children, the security team drank the Kool-Aid and perished. In total more than 900 people lost their lives to a man of questionable sanity and morals.

KOOL AID COOKIES

EAT THE KOOL AID COOKIES

INGREDIENTS

1 2/3 cups Sugar
1 1/4 cups butter
2 eggs
1/2 tsp salt
1 tsp baking soda
3 cups of flour
Kool-Aid in your choice of flavor(s)

1. Preheat the oven to 325 degrees.
2. In a mixer cream together butter and sugar.
3. Add eggs and mix well.
4. Add salt and baking soda.
5. Add flour to butter mixture 1/2 cup at a time and mix well.
6. If you would like more than flavor of cookies divide your dough into separate bowls now.
7. I divided my dough into four equal portions and used one half packet of Kool-Aid per portion. If you are making only two colors you will use one packet of Kool-Aid per half, if you only want one color use two packets for the entire recipe.
8. Mix Kool-Aid into dough until well blended and color is even.
9. Drop by rounded spoonfuls onto greased cookie sheet and bake 10-12 minutes.
10. Let cool one minute before removing from pan.

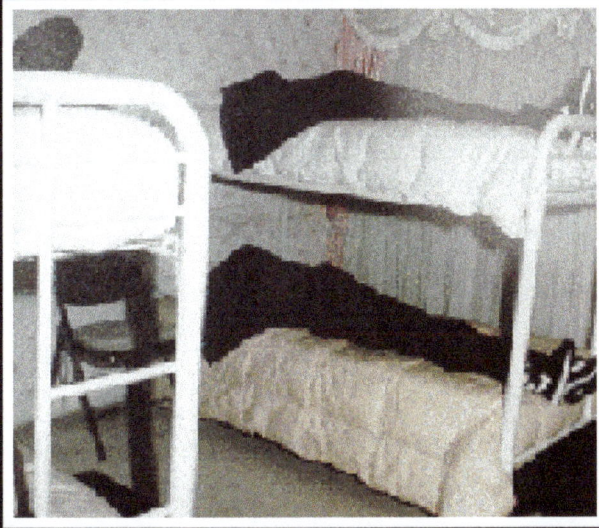

Heaven's Gate

Heaven's Gate, religious group founded in the United States on a belief in unidentified flying objects. Under a variety of names over the years, including Human Individual Metamorphosis, Bo and Peep, and Total Overcomers Anonymous, the group advocated extreme self-renunciation to the point of castration. It burst into public consciousness following the suicide of 39 of its members in a suburb of San Diego, California, in March 1997.

Founders Marshall H. Applewhite (1932–1997) and Bonnie Nettles (1927–1985) met in 1972 and soon became convinced that they were the two "endtime" witnesses mentioned in Revelation 11. In 1975 they held gatherings in California and Oregon that attracted their initial followers. Those who attached themselves to "The Two" dropped out of society and prepared for the "transition" to a new life on a spaceship.

When the expected transition did not occur, the group settled in Texas and lived a quiet communal existence practicing disciplines that they believed would prepare them for the eventual movement to a "higher level" of existence. They had few contacts with outsiders until 1994, when their expectation of the imminent transition was again heightened, and they began a new round of proselytization. They also divested themselves of most of their possessions and began a pilgrimage that led them to California.

Settling in the San Diego area in 1996, they supported themselves by creating sites on the World Wide Web for Internet users and established their own Web site to offer readers a gate to heaven (hence the name by which they would become known). Early in 1997 a rumour circulated among the New Age community that an artificial object, or spaceship, was following the recently discovered Comet Hale-Bopp, which would approach close to the Earth around the time of the spring equinox. As the comet approached, the Heaven's Gate group, which had shrunk to only 39 members, took poison in three waves of 15, 15, and 9 in the belief that the spaceship would arrive to take them to a better place.

BAKED HOT WINGS

HEAVEN'S HELLISHLY HOT WINGS

4 pounds chicken wings, halved at joints, wingtips discarded
2 Tablespoons baking powder*, aluminum free
3/4 teaspoon salt
1/2 teaspoon cracker black pepper
1 teaspoon paprika
1 teaspoon garlic powder

BUFFALO SAUCE:

1/3 cup Frank's Wings Hot Sauce
¼ cup Spicy BBQ sauce
Tabasco sauce to taste
1 1/2 cups light brown sugar
1 Tablespoon water

Other Sauce ideas: honey BBQ sauce, ranch, honey garlic sauce, BBQ sauce

INSTRUCTIONS

1. *Adjust your oven rack to the upper-middle position. Preheat oven to 425 degrees F.*
2. *Line a baking sheet with aluminum foil and place a wire rack (I use a cooling rack) on top. Spray the rack with non-stick spray.*
3. *Use paper towels to pat the wings dry and place them in a large bowl. It's important to dry them REALLY well!*
4. *Combine the salt, pepper, garlic powder, paprika, and baking powder in a small bowl. Then sprinkle the seasoning over the wings, tossing to evenly coat.*
5. *Arrange wings, skin side up, in single layer on prepared wire rack.*
6. *Bake on the upper middle oven rack, turning every 20 minutes until wings are crispy and browned. The total cook time will depend on the size of the wings but may take up to 1 hour.*
7. *Remove from oven and let stand for 5 minutes. Transfer wings to bowl and toss with sauce.*

FOR BUFFALO SAUCE:

1. *In a medium saucepan over medium heat stir together all sauce ingredients. Mix well until sugar has dissolved.*
2. *Remove from heat and allow to cool to room temperature before adding to wings (or prepare the sauce ahead of time and refrigerate*

Branch Davidians

Branch Davidian, member of an offshoot group of the Davidian Seventh-day Adventist Church that made headlines on February 28, 1993, when its Mount Carmel headquarters near Waco, Texas, was raided by the U.S. Bureau of Alcohol, Tobacco and Firearms (ATF); four federal agents were killed in the assault. A lengthy standoff between the group and government agents then followed. It ended on April 19, after some 80 members of the group, including their leader David Koresh, died when the Mount Carmel complex was burned to the ground following an attempted entrance by Federal Bureau of Investigation (FBI) agents.

One of the factions opposed to Florence Houteff's leadership was led by Ben Roden, who had previously called the Davidians to "Get off the dead Rod [led by Florence Houteff] and move to the living Branch." Roden gained control of Mount Carmel and established the General Association of Davidian Seventh-day Adventists. He called his members to a purer life and promised that Christ would return soon after the members reached a state of moral maturity. When Roden died in 1978, members were torn between allegiance to his wife, Lois, and his son, George. Lois found an ally in a young convert, Vernon Howell (1959–1993), but her death in 1986 left George in control. Within a year, however, Howell had asserted his leadership and become the head of the Mount Carmel community.

Howell moved quickly to assert his spiritual authority, and one of his first acts was the adoption of a new name, David Koresh. This name suggested that he was a spiritual heir of the biblical King David and that he, like Koresh (Hebrew for Cyrus, the ancient Persian king), was a messianic figure—though not the Messiah, Jesus. (Cyrus is the only non-Jew to whom the title *messiah*, or "anointed one," is given in Scripture.) Koresh exercised his new authority by taking several "spiritual" wives from among the group's unmarried members, and in 1989 he asserted that he was the perfect mate for all female members and confided to the Davidians his intention to create a new lineage of children who he believed would eventually rule the world.

CHUCK ROAST BURNT ENDS

DAVIDIANS BURNT BUILDINGS

- *3 pounds chuck roast*
- *2 Tablespoons yellow mustard*
- *1 Tablespoon each coarse salt, ground black pepper, and garlic powder*
- *¼ cup brown sugar*
- *2 Tablespoons brown sugar*

INSTRUCTIONS

1. **Preheat.** *Preheat your smoker for indirect grilling at 275 degrees F. Use hickory or oak wood for the most complementary smoke flavor.*
2. **Season.** Slather the chuck roast with yellow mustard then season liberally on all sides with Hey Grill Hey Beef Rub or equal parts salt, pepper, and garlic powder.
3. **Smoke.** When your smoker is up to temperature, place the seasoned roast on the smoker and close the lid. Smoke the roast until the internal temperature reaches 165 degrees F (this took 5 hours on my smoker). You should have a fairly nice dark bark on the exterior of your roast at this point.
4. **Wrap**. *Remove the roast from the grill and wrap it in either butcher paper or foil. Return the roast to the grill and continue smoking until the meat reaches an internal temperature of 195 degrees F (this took just over 1 hour).*
5. **Rest and cut.** Remove the wrapped roast from the grill and allow to rest for 15-20 minutes. Cut into 3/4 inch cubes and transfer to a foil baking pan.
6. **Add sauce.** *Sprinkle with 1/4 cup brown sugar and drizzle with most of the Everything BBQ sauce, reserving a couple of tablespoons for later. Toss gently to coat all of the pieces in a little of the sauce.*
7. **Finish smoking.** Place the pan on the grill, close the lid and cook for an additional 1 1/2 to 2 hours, or until the sauce is bubbly and the cubed bits of beef are falling apart tender.

NXIVM

NXIVM (/ˈnɛksiəm/ *NEK-see-əm*) was a cult led by convicted racketeer and sex offender Keith Raniere. NXIVM is also the name of the defunct company that Raniere founded in 1998, which provided seminars ostensibly about human potential development, and served as a front organization for criminal activity by Raniere and his close associates. Following Raniere›s conviction in 2019, the Department of Justice seized ownership of NXIVM-related entities and their intellectual property through asset forfeiture.

The NXIVM Corporation was based in the New York Capital District and had centers throughout the United States, Canada, and Mexico. The subsidiary companies of NXIVM recruited based on the multi-level marketing model and used curricula based on the intellectual property («tech») of Raniere called «Rational Inquiry». Courses attracted a variety of notable students including actors as well as the children of the rich and powerful. At its height, NXIVM had 700 active members.

Over its existence, former members and families of NXIVM clients, alarmed by Raniere's behavior and NXIVM's practices, spoke to investigative journalists of *Forbes*, *Vanity Fair*, *The New York Observer*, and the *Times Union* of Albany describing the organization as a cult. The organization was criticized in similar terms by Rick Alan Ross of the Cult Education Institute and activists and academics. In 2017, former members Sarah

Edmondson, Bonnie Piesse and Mark Vicente, as well as Catherine Oxenberg (mother of member India Oxenberg) spoke to *The New York Times* and revealed grave concerns about Keith Raniere and NXIVM, including the existence of a secret society called «DOS" in which women were branded, made to record false confessions and provide nude photographs for blackmail.

MULTI-LAYER FLAVORED CAKE

RAINIER'S MLM CAKE

There are 3 different cakes

PEANUT BUTTER CAKE

- *1 ⅔ cups (210 g) all-purpose flour*
- *3 tbsp (24 g) cornstarch*
- *½ tsp baking soda*
- *2 tsp baking powder*
- *½ tsp salt - omit if using salted butter*
- *⅓ cup (80 g) unsalted butter - room temperature*
- *⅓ cup (75 g) unflavored vegetable oil - I use canola oil*
- *½ cup (100 g) white granulated sugar*
- *¾ cup (150 g) soft brown sugar - in the US use light soft brown sugar*
- *⅔ cups (150 g) unsweetened peanut butter - use a creamy, processed one (see note 5 if using a sweetened version like Skippy)*
- *3 large eggs - room temperature*
- *1 ½ tsps vanilla extract/essence*
- *1 cup (225 g) buttermilk - room temperature*
- *To make a single layer cake, cut the ingredients in half*

102

PEANUT BUTTER FROSTING

- *1½ cups (340 g) unsalted butter - room temperature*
- *3 cups (375 g) powdered sugar - also known as icing or confectioners sugar*
- *2 tsps vanilla extract/essence*
- *½ cup (120 g) whipping or heavy cream - room temperature*
- *½ tsp salt*
- *1 cup (250 g) unsweetened peanut butter - use a creamy version*

Cook Mode *Prevent your screen from going dark*

INSTRUCTIONS

PEANUT BUTTER CAKE

- *Preheat oven to 180 °C (350°F) (see note 1 if using a fan function) and grease and/ or line two 8 inch cake tins. I use my homemade cake release to grease my tins.*
- *In a bowl, sift together flour, cornstarch, baking soda, baking powder and salt. Using a whisk or fork, mix until well combined. Set aside.*
- *In a large bowl, add in butter, vegetable oil, white granulated sugar, soft brown sugar and peanut butter. Using an electric mixer (hand or stand mixer are both fine - see note 2), cream together on a medium speed for 3 minutes until light and creamy.*
- *Add in eggs one at a time on a low speed, mixing well in between each addition (about 10-15 seconds between eggs).*
- *Add in vanilla and buttermilk, and mix on a medium speed until well combined. You should have a smooth creamy batter. Now set your mixer aside as the remainder of the batter will be finished by hand.*
- *Add in the pre-sifted dry ingredients from earlier and using a spatula, gently fold until just combined. Do not overmix (see note 3).*
- *Distribute the batter evenly into the two 8 inch cake tins, and drop the cake tins lightly on the counter to remove any large air bubbles. Bake for 30-35 minutes or until a toothpick comes out clean or with a few moist crumbs on it.*
- *Once baked, allow the cakes to cool in the cake tins for about 15-20 minutes, and then turn them out onto a wire rack to completely cool before frosting with the peanut butter frosting.*

PEANUT BUTTER FROSTING

- *Before beginning: If you're making a simple cake with no crumb coat, only a thin layer of frosting on the sides and little to no piping, you can get away with making a half batch (or 3/4s) of the frosting :)*
- *In a large bowl (or in the bowl of a stand mixer if using one), add in butter, powdered sugar, vanilla, cream, peanut butter and salt.*

- Mix on the lowest speed until the ingredients are combined (about a minute), and then turn up the speed to a medium high and mix for a full 10 minutes, scraping down the bowl half way through. If using a stand mixer then use the paddle attachment.
- The frosting should be silky smooth and it's now ready to use! See note 4 if your frosting isn't light and smooth, or too soft

BANANA CAKE

- 1 and 1/2 cups (345g) mashed bananas (about 4 medium or 3 large bananas)
- 3 cups (375g) all-purpose flour (spooned & leveled)
- 1 teaspoon baking powder
- 1 teaspoon baking soda
- 1/2 teaspoon ground cinnamon
- 1/2 teaspoon salt
- 3/4 cup (12 Tbsp; 170g) unsalted butter, softened to room temperature
- 1 cup (200g) granulated sugar
- 1/2 cup (100g) packed light or dark brown sugar
- 3 large eggs, at room temperature
- 2 teaspoons pure vanilla extract
- 1 and 1/2 cups (360ml) buttermilk, at room temperature*
- To make a single layer cake, cut the ingredients in half

CREAM CHEESE FROSTING

- 8 ounces (226g) full-fat brick **cream cheese**, softened to room temperature
- 1/2 cup (8 Tbsp; 113g) unsalted butter, softened to room temperature
- 3 cups (360g) confectioners' sugar, plus an extra 1/4 cup if needed
- 1 teaspoon pure vanilla extract
- 1/8 teaspoon salt

Cook Mode Prevent your screen from going dark

INSTRUCTIONS

1. Preheat the oven to 350°F (177°C) and grease a 9×13-inch pan.
2. **Make the cake:** Mash the bananas. I usually just use my mixer for this! Set mashed bananas aside.
3. Whisk the flour, baking powder, baking soda, cinnamon, and salt together. Set aside.
4. Using a handheld or stand mixer fitted with a paddle attachment, beat the butter on high speed until smooth and creamy—about 1 minute. Add both sugars and beat on high speed for 2 minutes until creamed together. Scrape down the sides and up the bottom of the bowl with a rubber spatula as needed. Add the eggs and the vanilla. Beat on medium-high speed until combined, then beat in the

mashed bananas. Scrape down the sides and up the bottom of the bowl as needed. With the mixer on low speed, add the dry ingredients in three additions alternating with the buttermilk and mixing each addition just until incorporated. Do not overmix. The batter will be slightly thick and a few lumps is OK.

5. Spread batter into the prepared pan. Bake for 45–50 minutes. Baking times vary, so keep an eye on yours. The cake is done when a toothpick inserted in the center comes out clean. If you find the top of the cake is browning too quickly in the oven, loosely cover it with aluminum foil.

6. Remove the cake from the oven and set on a wire rack. Allow to cool completely. After about 45 minutes, I usually place it in the refrigerator to speed things up.

7. **Make the frosting:** In a large bowl using a handheld or stand mixer fitted with a paddle or whisk attachment, beat the cream cheese and butter together on high speed until smooth and creamy. Add 3 cups confectioners' sugar, vanilla, and salt. Beat on low speed for 30 seconds, then switch to high speed and beat for 2 minutes. If you want the frosting a little thicker, add the extra 1/4 cup of confectioners sugar (I add it). Spread the frosting on the cooled cake. Refrigerate for 30 minutes before serving. This helps sets the frosting and makes cutting easier.

8. Cover leftover cake tightly and store in the refrigerator for 5 days.

CHOCOLATE CAKE

- 1 and 3/4 cups (219g) all-purpose flour (spooned & leveled)
- 3/4 cup (62g) unsweetened natural cocoa powder
- 1 and 3/4 cups (350g) granulated sugar
- 2 teaspoons baking soda
- 1 teaspoon baking powder
- 1 teaspoon salt
- 2 teaspoons espresso powder (optional)
- 1/2 cup (120ml) vegetable oil (or canola oil or melted coconut oil)
- 2 large eggs, at room temperature
- 2 teaspoons pure vanilla extract
- To make one cake cut the ingredients, in half.
- 1 cup (240ml) buttermilk, at room temperature
- 1 cup (240ml) freshly brewed strong hot coffee (regular or decaf)

CHOCOLATE BUTTERCREAM

- 1 and 1/4 cups (282g) unsalted butter, softened to room temperature
- 3 and 1/2 cups (420g) confectioners' sugar
- 3/4 cup (65g) unsweetened cocoa powder (natural or dutch process)
- 3–5 Tablespoons (45-75ml) heavy cream (or half-and-half or milk), at room temperature
- 1/4 teaspoon salt
- 1 teaspoon pure vanilla extract
- optional for decoration: semi-sweet chocolate chips

INSTRUCTIONS

1. *Preheat oven to 350°F (177°C). Grease two 9-inch cake pans, line with parchment paper rounds, then grease the parchment paper. Parchment paper helps the cakes seamlessly release from the pans. (If it's helpful, see this parchment paper rounds for cakes video & post.)*

2. **Make the cake:** *Whisk the flour, cocoa powder, sugar, baking soda, baking powder, salt, and espresso powder (if using) together in a large bowl. Set aside. Using a handheld or stand mixer fitted with a whisk attachment (or you can use a whisk) mix the oil, eggs, and vanilla together on medium-high speed until combined. Add the buttermilk and mix until combined. Pour the wet ingredients into the dry ingredients, add the hot water/coffee, and whisk or beat on low speed until the batter is completely combined. Batter is thin.*

3. *Divide batter evenly between pans. Bake for 23-26 minutes or until a toothpick inserted in the center comes out clean. Baking times vary, so keep an eye on yours. The cakes are done when a toothpick inserted in the center comes out clean. (**Note:** Even if they're completely done, the cooled cakes may *slightly* sink in the center. Cocoa powder is simply not as structurally strong as all-purpose flour and can't hold up to all the moisture necessary to make a moist tasting chocolate cake. It's normal!)*

4. *Remove the cakes from the oven and set on a wire rack. Allow to cool completely in the pan*

5. **Make the buttercream:** *With a handheld or stand mixer fitted with a paddle attachment, beat the butter on medium speed until creamy—about 2 minutes. Add confectioners' sugar, cocoa powder, 3 Tablespoons heavy cream, salt, and vanilla extract. Beat on low speed for 30 seconds, then increase to high speed and beat for 1 full minute. Do not over-whip. Add 1/4 cup more confectioners' sugar or cocoa powder if frosting is too thin or 1-2 more Tablespoons of cream if frosting is too thick. (I usually add 1 more.) Taste. Add another pinch of salt if desired.*

6. **Assemble and frost:** *If cooled cakes are domed on top, use a large serrated knife to slice a thin layer off the tops to create a flat surface. This is called "leveling" the cakes. Discard or crumble over finished cake. Place 1 cake layer on your cake stand or serving plate. Evenly cover the top with frosting. Top with 2nd layer and spread remaining frosting all over the top and sides. I always use an icing spatula and bench scraper for the frosting. Garnish with chocolate chips, if desired.*

7. *Refrigerate uncovered cake for at least 30-60 minutes before slicing to help set the shape. After that, you can serve the cake or continue refrigerating for up to 4–6 hours before serving. Cake can be served at room temperature or chilled.*

8. *Cover leftover cake tightly and store in the refrigerator for 5 days. I like using a cake carrier for storing.*

To make the multi-layer cake start with the chocolate on the bottom. Frost the center with the plain buttercream. Then the banana butter cream, more frosting and top with the peanut butter. Frost the top and sides. Keep in the refrigerator.

Angels Landing

The Angel's Landing cult was led by Daniel Perez, also known as Lou Castro, who convinced his followers that he had supernatural powers and was an angel. The cult was based on a 20-acre property near Wichita, Kansas. Perez manipulated his followers, claiming he needed to have sex with children to survive, and he was involved in multiple crimes, including sexual abuse and murder.

Perez was convicted in 2015 of numerous charges, including rape, child exploitation, and the murder of a follower named Patricia Hughes. He also collected millions of dollars in life insurance payouts from the deaths of his followers.

Daniel Perez used a combination of manipulation, charisma, and deceit to convince people to join his cult. Some examples of how he convinced people and parents to do the unthinkable were; claiming Supernatural Powers: Perez convinced his followers that he was an angel who could see the future and heal the sick. He claimed to be hundreds or even thousands of years old. Creating a Sense of Community: He established a close-knit community on a 20-acre property called Angel's Landing, where followers felt a sense of belonging and purpose. Exploiting Vulnerabilities: Perez preyed on people's emotional and psychological vulnerabilities. He often targeted individuals who were going through difficult times or who were searching for meaning in their lives. Using Fear and Control:

He maintained control over his followers through fear, claiming that he needed to have sex with children to survive and threatening those who resisted. Financial Manipulation: Perez also manipulated his followers financially, taking out life insurance policies on them and collecting the payouts when they died under suspicious circumstances.

In the end Perez was sentenced to life in prison for his many violent, manipulative, and heinous crimes. He is currently serving his sentence at Lansing County Correctional Facility in Kansas.

ANGEL FOOD CAKE

FALLEN ANGEL CAKE

INGREDIENTS

- 1 and 3/4 cups (350g) **granulated sugar***
- 1 cup + 2 Tablespoons (133g) **cake flour**
- 1/4 teaspoon **salt**
- 12 large **egg whites**, at room temperature*
- 1 and 1/2 teaspoons **cream of tartar**
- 1 and 1/2 teaspoons **pure vanilla extract**
- 1 teaspoon of almond extract

INSTRUCTIONS

1. *Adjust the oven rack to the lower middle position and preheat oven to 325°F (163°C).*
2. *In a food processor or blender, pulse the sugar until fine and powdery. Remove 1 cup and set aside to use in step 3; keep the rest inside the food processor. Add the cake flour and salt to the food processor. Pulse 5-10 times until sugar/flour/salt mixture is aerated and light.*
3. *In a large bowl using a hand mixer or a stand mixer fitted with a whisk attachment, whip egg whites and cream of tartar together on medium-low until foamy, about 1 minute. Switch to medium-high and slowly add the 1 cup of sugar you set aside. Whip until soft peaks form, about 5-6 minutes. Add the vanilla extract, then beat just until incorporated.*
4. *In 3 additions, slowly sift the flour mixture into the egg white mixture using a fine mesh strainer, gently folding with a rubber spatula after each addition. To avoid deflating or a dense cake, don't add the flour mixture all at once. Sift and very slowly fold in several additions. This is important! Pour and spread batter into*

an **ungreased** 9 or 10 inch tube pan. Shimmy the pan on the counter to smooth down the surface.

5. *Bake the cake until a toothpick inserted comes out clean, about 40-45 minutes. Rotate the pan halfway through baking. The cake will rise up very tall while baking. Remove from the oven, then cool the cake completely upside-down set on a wire rack, about 3 hours. (Upside-down so the bottom of the tube pan is right-side up, see photo and video above.) Once cooled, run a thin knife around the edges and gently tap the pan on the counter until the cake releases.*

6. *If desired, dust with confectioners' sugar. Slice the cake with a sharp serrated knife. Regular knives can easily squish the cake. Serve with whipped cream and fresh berries.*

Children of God

Children of God is a religious group that originated in California in 1968. Because its leaders have historically limited members' access to the outside world and asked them to give up their money and worldly possessions, Children of God is generally considered a cult. The group became notorious when news stories emerged accusing its members of sexually abusing children

The cult's early beginnings are rooted in the counterculture movement of the late 1960s. Founder David Brandt Berg, a pastor and evangelist for the Christian and Missionary Alliance, became the leader of a youth ministry called Teen Challenge in Huntington Beach, California, in 1967. Berg recruited his group's members out of the hippies and outcasts that flocked to southern California during the "free love" era and organized a group of young people to roam the streets proselytizing about the love of Jesus.

Following a trial relating to the custody of a child born into the cult, the Rt. Hon. Lord Justice Ward wrote a 295-page opinion on The Family. Ward determined that the group had permitted sexual abuse of minors, deliberately isolated and sequestered children away from their parents, and used extensive corporal punishment. Ward also concluded that by the time of the trial, these practices had ceased, and that he believed The Family was not presently an unsafe environment for children.

The Family International is still an active group. Former members continue to speak up about the abuse they faced during their time in the cult. The Family International has, since 1989, officially condemned sexual acts with minors and is not currently considered a threat to children by law enforcement.

CORNBREAD

CHILDREN OF CORNBREAD

Ingredients *Oven 400 degrees*

- *1 cup (120g) fine cornmeal*
- *1 cup (125g) all-purpose flour (spooned & leveled)*
- *1 teaspoon baking powder*
- *1/2 teaspoon baking soda*
- *1/8 teaspoon salt*
- *1/2 cup (8 Tbsp; 113g) unsalted butter, melted and slightly cooled*
- *1/3 cup (67g) packed light or dark brown sugar*
- *2 Tablespoons (30ml) honey*
- *1 large egg, at room temperature*
- *1 can cream of corn*
- *1/2 cup (240ml) buttermilk, at room temperature**

INSTRUCTIONS

1. *Preheat oven to 400°F (204°C). Grease and lightly flour a 9-inch square baking pan. Set aside.*
2. *Whisk the cornmeal, flour, baking powder, baking soda, and salt together in a large bowl. Set aside. In a medium bowl, whisk the melted butter, brown sugar, and honey together until completely smooth and thick. Then, whisk in the egg until combined. Finally, whisk in the buttermilk. Pour the wet ingredients into the dry ingredients and whisk until combined. Avoid over-mixing.*
3. *Pour batter into prepared baking pan. Bake for 20 minutes or until golden brown on top and the center is cooked through. Use a toothpick to test. Edges should be crispy at this point. Allow to slightly cool before slicing and serving. Serve cornbread with butter, honey, jam, or whatever you like.*

Matamoros: Los Narcosatanicos

Adolfo de Jesús Constanzo (November 1, 1962 – May 6, 1989) was a Cuban-American serial killer, drug dealer and cult leader who led an infamous drug-trafficking and occult gang in Matamoros, Tamaulipas, Mexico, that was dubbed the Narcosatanists (Spanish: *Los Narcosatánicos*) by the media. His cult members nicknamed him **The Godfather** (*El Padrino*). Constanzo led the cult with Sara Aldrete, whom followers nicknamed "The Godmother" (*La Madrina*). The cult was involved in multiple ritualistic killings in Matamoros, including the murder of Mark Kilroy, an American student abducted, tortured and killed in the area in 1989.

Constanzo began to believe that his magic, much of which he took from Palo Mayombe, was responsible for the success of the cartels and demanded to become a full business partner with one of the most powerful families he knew, the Calzadas. When his demand was rejected, seven family members disappeared. Their bodies turned up later with fingers, toes, ears, brains and even (in one case) the spine missing. Constanzo soon made friends with a new cartel, the Hernandez brothers. He also took up with a young woman named Sara Aldrete, who became the high priestess of the cult. Constanzo made Aldrete second-in-command of his cult and directed her to supervise his followers while he was shipping marijuana over the border into the US.

On March 13, 1989, Constanzo's henchmen abducted a pre-med student, Mark Kilroy, from outside a Mexican bar and took him back to the ranch. Kilroy was a US citizen who had been in Mexico on spring break. When Kilroy was brought to the ranch, Constanzo murdered him. Under pressure from Texan politicians, Mexican police initially picked up four of Constanzo's followers, including two of the Hernandez brothers. Police quickly discovered the cult and that Constanzo had been responsible for Kilroy's death; he sought a "good"/superior brain" for one of his ritual spells. Officers raided the ranch and discovered Constanzo's cauldron, which contained various items such as a dead black cat and a human brain. Fifteen mutilated corpses were dug up at the ranch, one of them Kilroy's. Officials said Kilroy was killed by Constanzo with a machete chop to the back of the neck when Kilroy tried to escape about 12 hours after being taken to the ranch.

SPAGHETTI WITH MEAT MARINARA

ODE TO MATAMOROS

RITUAL SPAGHETTI SACRIFICE

INGREDIENTS

- 1 pound ground beef (or 1/2 lb ground Italian sausage and 1/2 lb ground beef)
- salt and freshly ground black pepper, to taste
- 1 medium onion, chopped
- 15 ounces tomato sauce
- 6 ounces tomato paste
- 1/2 teaspoon Italian seasoning
- 1 Tablespoon dried parsley flakes
- 1 teaspoon garlic powder
- crushed red pepper flakes, to taste
- 1 Tablespoon Worcestershire sauce
- 1 Tablespoon granulated sugar
- 1 cup water
- 1/4 cup fresh basil leaves (optional)
- spaghetti noodles, for serving
- 1 pound ground beef (or 1/2 lb ground Italian sausage and 1/2 lb ground beef)
- salt and freshly ground black pepper, to taste
- 1 medium onion, chopped

- *15 ounces tomato sauce*
- *6 ounces tomato paste*
- *1/2 teaspoon Italian seasoning*
- *1 Tablespoon dried parsley flakes*
- *1 teaspoon garlic powder*
- *crushed red pepper flakes, to taste*
- *1 Tablespoon Worcestershire sauce*
- *1 Tablespoon granulated sugar*
- *1 cup water*
- *1/4 cup fresh basil leaves (optional)*
- *spaghetti noodles, for serving*

INSTRUCTIONS

1. *Season ground beef with salt and pepper.*
2. *In a large skillet, add the beef and chopped onion and brown. Drain excess grease.*
3. *Add tomato sauce, tomato paste, Italian seasoning, parsley, garlic powder, crushed red pepper, Worcestershire, and sugar to the skillet.*
4. *Stir well to combine and bring to a boil. Add water and stir well.*
5. *Reduce heat and simmer for 30 minutes. Add chopped basil before serving, if desired.*

Order of the Solar Temple

The Order of the Solar Temple (French: Ordre du Temple solaire, OTS), or simply the Solar Temple, was an esoteric new religious movement and secret society, often described as a cult, notorious for the mass deaths of many of its members in several incidents throughout the 1990s. The OTS was a neo-Templar movement, claiming to be a continuation of the Knights Templar, and incorporated a mix of Rosicrucianism, Theosophy, and New Age ideas. It was led by Joseph Di Mambro, with Luc Jouret as a spokesman and second in command. It was founded in 1984, in Geneva, Switzerland.

Following increasing legal and media scandal, including investigations over arms trafficking and pressure from an ex-member, as well as conflict within the group, the founders began to prepare for what they described as "transit" to the star Sirius. In 1994, they first ordered the murder of a family of ex-members in Quebec, before orchestrating mass suicide and mass murder on two communes in Switzerland. In the following years, there were two other mass suicides of former OTS members in France in 1995 and in Quebec in 1997; in total, 74 people died in the course of these events, the classification of which as either mass suicide or mass murder is disputed. The OTS was a major factor in the toughening of the fight against cults in France.

In 1995, the OTS was listed as a cult in the report of the Parliamentary Commission on Cults in France. The group's actions were a major factor in the toughening of the fight against cults in France. In the wake of the deaths, fear of cults took hold of the French and Swiss populations. The acts of the Solar Temple prompted European governments to begin to monitor new and nontraditional religious movements, and also influenced the American anti-cult movement.

In the aftermath, many anti-cult activists compared Jouret — viewed then as the charismatic leader of the OTS — to David Koresh, though Di Mambro was later described as the group's main leader, with Jouret its recruiter.

MONTE CRISTO SANDWICH

KNIGHTS TEMPLAR OR MAYBE MONTE CRISTO

INGREDIENTS

- 2 slices bread
- 1 teaspoon mayonnaise
- 1 teaspoon prepared mustard
- 2 slices cooked ham
- 2 slices cooked turkey meat
- 1 slice Swiss cheese
- 1 large egg
- ½ cup milk

DIRECTIONS

1. Gather all ingredients.
2. Spread mayonnaise on one side of one bread slice. Spread mustard on one side of remaining bread slice.
3. Top with alternate slices of ham, turkey, and Swiss cheese.
4. Close sandwich with remaining bread slice, mayonnaise-side down.
5. Beat egg and milk in a shallow bowl until well combined. Lightly grease a small skillet over medium heat.
6. Dip sandwich into egg mixture to coat on both sides.
7. Transfer sandwich to the hot skillet and cook until golden brown on both sides and cheese is melted.
8. Serve hot.

Movement for the Restoration of the Ten Commandments of God

The Movement for the Restoration of the Ten Commandments of God (MRTC or MRTCG) was a religious movement founded by Credonia Mwerinde and Joseph Kibweteere in southwestern Uganda, notorious for the mass death of several hundred members of the group in a mass suicide in the year 2000. It was formed in 1989 after Mwerinde and Kibweteere claimed that they had seen visions of the Virgin Mary.

On 17 March 2000, followers of the religious movement died in a fire and a series of poisonings and killings, which were initially considered a mass suicide. That initial suspicion was revised to mass murder when hundreds of other bodies were discovered in pits at sites related to the movement that had died at least weeks prior to the event; the official conclusion was a mass murder, though this has been disputed by other commentators who argue that it was actually a mass suicide. Over 300 people died in the fire, while over 400 were discovered in the pits.

The Movement held a huge party at Kanungu, where they roasted three bulls and drank 70 crates of soft drinks (most being Coca-Cola). Minutes after the members arrived at the party, nearby villagers heard an explosion, and the building was gutted in an intense fire that killed all 530 in attendance. The windows and doors of the building had been boarded up to prevent people from leaving.

The fire alerted the Ugandan authorities as to what had been occurring in the Movement. Several days before, Movement leader Dominic Kataribabo had been seen buying 50 liters of sulfuric acid, which may have started the fire. Another party was planned for the eighteenth, which officials believe sect leaders had announced in order to mislead authorities as to their plans. The whereabouts of the five principal cult leaders Joseph Kibweteere, Joseph Kasapurari, John Kamagara, Dominic Kataribabo, and Credonia Mwerinde are unknown (all having presumably escaped).

CHILI AND CORNBREAD

FIRE AND BRIMSTONE CHILI AND CORNBREAD

INGREDIENTS

- 1 tablespoon olive oil
- 1 yellow onion, diced
- 2 teaspoons kosher salt, or more to taste
- 2 pounds ground beef
- 2 tablespoons all-purpose flour
- ½ cup diced poblano pepper
- 3 cloves garlic, crushed
- 3 tablespoons chili powder
- 2 teaspoons ground cumin
- 2 teaspoons freshly ground black pepper
- ½ teaspoon cayenne pepper
- ½ teaspoon dried oregano
- 1 (15 ounce) can fire-roasted diced tomatoes
- 1 (15 ounce) can fire-roasted crushed tomatoes
- 2 cups water, or as needed
- 1 (16 ounce) can kidney beans, rinsed and drained

FOR THE CORNBREAD CRUST:

- 2 (7.5 ounce) packages corn muffin mix (such as Jiffy®)
- 1 cup grated white Cheddar cheese, divided
- 2 large eggs
- 1 cup milk

GARNISH:

- ¼ cup sour cream, or to taste
- ¼ cup chopped fresh cilantro, or to taste

DIRECTIONS

1. Heat oil in a large pot over high heat. Add onion, salt, and ground beef. Cook and stir with a wooden spoon or spatula until meat is browned and crumbled into small pieces, about 5 minutes. Stir in flour and cook for 2 minutes. Add poblano pepper, garlic, chili powder, cumin, black pepper, cayenne, and oregano; cook, stirring, for 2 to 3 minutes.
2. Stir in diced tomatoes and crushed tomatoes. Measure water using the empty tomato cans and pour into the pot. Bring to a simmer, stirring occasionally, then reduce heat to medium-low. Let simmer, stirring occasionally, for 30 minutes before stirring in kidney beans. Continue simmering until bubbling and fragrant, about 30 minutes more. Taste for seasoning and adjust.
3. Preheat the oven to 400 degrees F (200 degrees C).
4. Place a deep 9x13-inch baking dish on a baking sheet. Transfer chili to the dish, being sure to leave at least 1 inch of space at the top. Stir to evenly distribute.
5. Whisk corn muffin mix, 1/2 of the Cheddar cheese, eggs, and milk together in a bowl until smooth. Spoon evenly over chili until the surface is covered. Sprinkle with remaining Cheddar cheese.
6. Bake in the preheated oven until cornbread crust is browned and a toothpick inserted into the crust comes out clean, about 30 minutes.

Aum Shinrikyo

Aum Shinrikyo (オウム真理教, Oumu Shinrikyō, literally 'religion of Aum Supreme Truth'), is a Japanese new religious movement and doomsday cult founded by Shoko Asahara in 1987. It carried out the deadly Tokyo subway sarin attack in 1995 and was found to have been responsible for the Matsumoto sarin attack the previous year.

The group says that those who carried out the attacks did so secretly, without their plans being known to other executives and ordinary believers. Asahara insisted on his innocence in a radio broadcast relayed from Russia and directed toward Japan.[2]

On the morning of 20 March 1995, Aum members released a binary chemical weapon, most closely chemically similar to sarin, in a coordinated attack on five trains in the Tokyo subway system, killing 13 commuters, seriously injuring 54 and affecting 980 more. Some estimates claim as many as 6,000 people were injured by the sarin. It is difficult to obtain exact numbers since many victims are reluctant to come forward

On 6 July 2018, after exhausting all appeals, Asahara and six followers on death row were executed as punishment for the 1995 attacks and other crimes. Six additional followers were executed on 26 July. At 12:10 am, on New Year's Day 2019, at least nine people were injured (one seriously) when a car was deliberately driven into crowds celebrating the new year on Takeshita Street in Tokyo. Local police reported the arrest of Kazuhiro Kusakabe, the suspected driver, who allegedly admitted to intentionally ramming his vehicle into crowds to protest his opposition to the death penalty, specifically in retaliation for the execution of the aforementioned Aum cult members.

TERIYAKI CHICKEN

ODE TO AUM SHINRIKYO

SARIN CHICKEN

INGREDIENTS

- ½ cup white sugar
- ½ cup soy sauce
- ¼ cup cider vinegar
- 1 tablespoon cornstarch
- 1 tablespoon cold water
- 1 clove garlic, minced
- ½ teaspoon ground ginger
- ¼ teaspoon ground black pepper
- 12 boneless, skinless chicken thighs

DIRECTIONS

1. Preheat the oven to 425 degrees F (220 degrees C). Lightly grease a 9x13-inch baking dish.
2. Combine sugar, soy sauce, cider vinegar, cornstarch, cold water, garlic, ginger, and pepper in a small saucepan over low heat. Simmer, stirring frequently, until teriyaki sauce thickens and bubbles, 3 to 5 minutes. Remove from the heat.
3. Place chicken thighs in the prepared baking dish. Brush both sides of each thigh with the sauce. Reserve any extra sauce for basting.
4. Bake in the preheated oven for 30 minutes.
5. Flip chicken and brush with sauce. Continue to bake, basting with remaining sauce every 10 minutes, until no longer pink and juices run clear, 20 to 30 more minutes.